Sailing
"The Annapolis Way"

Sailing
"The Annapolis Way"

*How to master the basic techniques for
ocean, lake, and river, as taught
at the nation's famous sailing school*

Captain Ernie Barta

Illustrations by Lisa Kennedy

Stackpole Books

Published by
STACKPOLE BOOKS
Cameron and Kelker Streets
P.O. Box 1831
Harrisburg, PA 17105

Printed in the U.S.A.

Library of Congress Cataloging in Publication Data

Barta, Ernie.
  Sailing "the Annapolis way".

  1. Sailing.   2. Sailing – Study and teaching – United States.   I. Title.
GV811.5.B37 1984   797.1'24'07   84-51
ISBN 0-8117-2262-7

To Ann

Contents

8 / Contents

Preface

When the wind is blowing and the sun is shining, it is very difficult to sit down and write. If it weren't for the help of the Annapolis Sailing School's® entire organization – from Kathy and Jerry Wood all the way down to the boat cleaners – this book would never have been produced.

I must offer very special thanks to Jeff Holland, who has taken my sometimes fractured English and made it into a readable instruction book – and, of course, Lisa Kennedy, who has worked so hard and long on the illustrations. Together, I feel we have created a book that can help the beginning sailor progress, with our skill and knowledge behind him, from the novice level to a reasonable degree of sailing skill.

I sincerely hope that the combined efforts of all of these very knowledgeable people will help you to become a skilled and safe sailor.

Introduction

This book is intended for the first-time sailor who has either just purchased his boat or is learning on a friend's boat. It can also be a great help to an experienced sailor as a text and as a lesson plan in teaching a friend to sail.

Sailing "The Annapolis Way", like the Annapolis Sailing School®, teaches hands-on sailing. In many areas of the world, qualified instruction is simply not available. Although instructors can teach you faster, easier, and far more safely than you can teach yourself, this book can help you stumble through some areas without the aid of a trained instructor.

Many times during the text we will warn you: *Please do not attempt to do this without somebody in the boat who has had at least a minimum of sailing experience.* Heed this advice. In sailing, it's what you *don't* know that can get you into the most trouble.

"The Annapolis Way" has been used successfully for twenty-five years to teach people to sail in keel boats of approximately 24 feet. The purpose of this book is to teach people with small centerboard boats, larger swing-keel boats, or full-keeled boats up to 28 feet long. We will make no attempt to teach board sailing—although all of the aerodynamic principles apply. We will make no attempt to teach racing—although racing is just getting from point A to point B rapidly. And if you are sailing your boat properly, you are sailing it rapidly.

This book is set up in seven major parts. After each of these parts, you will find review questions to test your skill. A practice session in the boat will then help solidify the theory you have learned by reading and studying the text and the review questions. You can then go to the next section with a logical, step-by-step development of your sailing skills.

Parts 5 and 7 cover information that can be learned ashore and practiced ashore. If you happen to be in Wisconsin in January, sit in front of your fireplace, put your feet up, and start on these sections. By the time the weather turns nice in the spring, you'll have them firmly under your belt. As your skills increase from section to section, you can perform the maneuvers under more trying conditions. Finally, you will be able to handle most of them quite well singlehandedly.

Needless to say, we feel the fastest and safest way to learn to sail is with a certified sailing school and sailing instructor. However, with patience and fortitude, you can learn to sail using this book alone. After all, Columbus learned to sail the hard way, and look how far he got.

1

Starting Out

WHY A BOAT SAILS

Before we start learning how to sail, we must learn why a boat sails so that we can make intelligent decisions about how to set our sails and why to set them that way. A sailboat sails downwind for one very simple reason: the wind pushes it downwind. The first man who sat on a log raft and held up a leafy branch went downwind, but he had to swim or walk back. The large square-riggers developed in the fifteenth century were pretty good at sailing downwind, across the wind, and sometimes barely into the wind, but not as efficiently as a modern sailboat.

A boat sails into the wind for the same reason that an airplane flies. We must have an airfoil shape to the sails to create a difference in air pressure between one side of the sail and the other. The speed of the wind passing over the airfoil structure of the sail creates a low-pressure area in front of the sail and a high-pressure area in back of it. The boat and the sail are actually sucked into this low-pressure area, moving the boat ahead. If it weren't for a centerboard or keel underneath, the boat would slide sideways rather than move forward.

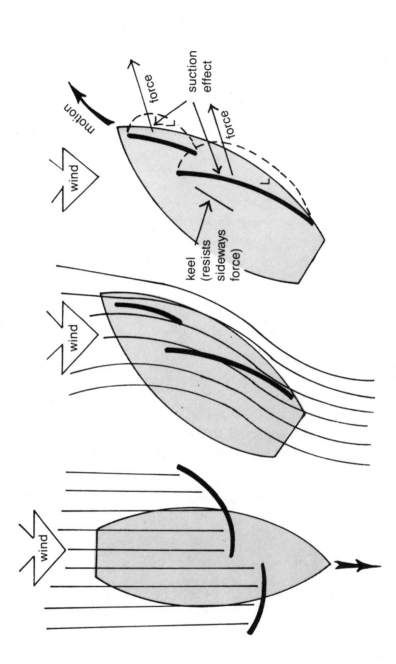

When the wind is behind you, the boat is just pushed downwind; but when you sail into the wind, the airfoil shape of the sail creates a suction effect moving the boat forward.

There are three things needed to make the boat sail into the wind:

(1) An airfoil shape to the sail. Sails are not flat. They have an airfoil shape built into them by the sailmaker.
(2) A keel or centerboard to keep the boat from sliding sideways. This is put into the boat by the designer and builder.
(3) A difference in air pressure on either side of the sail. This is produced by the wind with the help of the helmsman – you – in steering the boat in the proper direction and setting the sails the correct way.

I cannot emphasize this enough: without all three – airfoil shape to the sail, keel or centerboard to keep the boat from sliding sideways, and a difference in air pressure on either side of the sails – a boat will not sail.

TYPES OF SAILBOATS

There are as many types of sailboats manufactured today as there are types of automobiles. The three chief kinds of hulls are centerboard, swing keel, and fixed keel.

The centerboard type can be broken down into three distinct categories: centerboards, daggerboards, and leeboards. A centerboard boat has a large flat board which swings up into a well in the hull of the boat and is usually raised or lowered by cable. A daggerboard boat has a daggerboard which slides up and down in a well and is usually raised by hand. On a boat with leeboards, such as inland lake scows, there are two wells – one located on either side of the center of the boat – into which these boards hinge up and down. In the case of a small pramlike boat, the leeboards are attached directly to the sides of the boat and hinge up and down.

The purpose of these centerboards, daggerboards, and leeboards is identical. There only function is to keep the boat from sliding sideways through the water. In order for a boat to sail towards the wind, or to windward, the boat must have some method to keep it from sideslipping.

Swing keels serve two functions. Unlike the centerboard, which just keeps the boat from sliding sideways, the swing keel is ballasted, which provides stability. When the swing keel is lowered, its large area keeps the boat from sliding sideways, and its heavy weight keeps the wind in the sails from capsizing the boat.

The swing keel is a rather recent development, and a good one, since it has allowed thousands of people to trailer larger, stabler boats

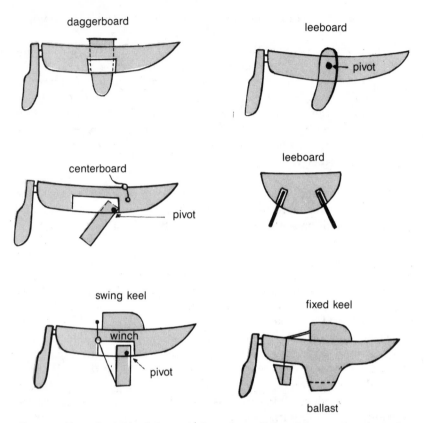

All types of boards and keels keep the boat from sliding sideways, but the swing keel, when lowered, and the fixed keel promote stability as well.

than before. When the swing keel is raised, the boat has a very shallow draft and can be easily loaded onto a trailer.

Many beginners make the mistake of sailing a swing-keel boat with the keel either halfway up or all the way up. This is not the purpose of the swing keel. A swing-keel boat should always be sailed with the keel in the down position. The keel is raised only for trailering.

A fixed-keel boat has a large permanant keel, heavily ballasted, which – like the swing keel – serves two purposes. It keeps the boat from sliding sideways and it promotes stability. The fixed-keel boat has neither the ability to go into shallow water nor to go easily onto a trailer, as a swing-keel boat can. But in many parts of the country, a fixed-keel boat is desirable because of its stability, strength, and resulting safety.

RIGGING

One of the most confusing things to a beginning sailor is understanding the language of sailing. It's almost as if you were going into a foreign country and having to learn a new language. Throughout this book we will try to use the simplest terms. However, there are parts of the boat that you must learn so that we can tell you what to do with them.

First, there is the hull, or the main body, of the boat. Almost all boats today are made of some sort of fiberglass-reinforced plastic and have a keel or centerboard attached. The front of the boat – or the pointy end, as some people call it – is the bow. And the back, or round end, is the stern. One difficulty in sailing is that people will cause confusion by saying "Go forward" or "Go to the bow," using two terms for exactly the same command. You must learn as much of the nautical language as you can. If you use it in your everyday speech, it will soon become second nature.

There's the starboard, or right-hand side of the boat, and the port, or left-hand side of the boat. The tiller is the stick with which you steer the boat. It is attached to the rudder, which causes the boat to steer. And the tiller, of course, is located in the cockpit, where you sit, just as if you were in the cockpit of an airplane.

The mast and the boom are usually aluminum extrusions to which you attach your sails. The mast is vertical, like a flagpole, and the boom sticks out horizontally from the mast. There's an old story that the boom got its name from the noise it makes when it hits your head. That's not true because, with today's aluminum booms, we would have to call them "clunks."

The boom is attached to the mast by a gooseneck. The gooseneck is nothing more than a universal joint which allows the boom to swing to the right and left, and also to move up and down. At the end of the boom, opposite the gooseneck, is the mainsheet. Here we have another conflict in nautical language. A sail is not a sheet. A sheet is a rope which attaches to the boom or the sail and allows you to adjust the sail properly. A sail is a sail; a piece of rope or line that trims a sail is a sheet. Don't feel bad if, up to this point in your life, you've called a sail a sheet. In one of his early novels, one of our Nobel Prize–winning novelists wrote: "The young lady was relaxing in the cockpit in the shade of the mainsheet." It must have been either a very thin woman or a very fat piece of rope.

The mast is held upright through a series of stays and shrouds. The forestay extends from the top of the mast to the bow of the boat; the

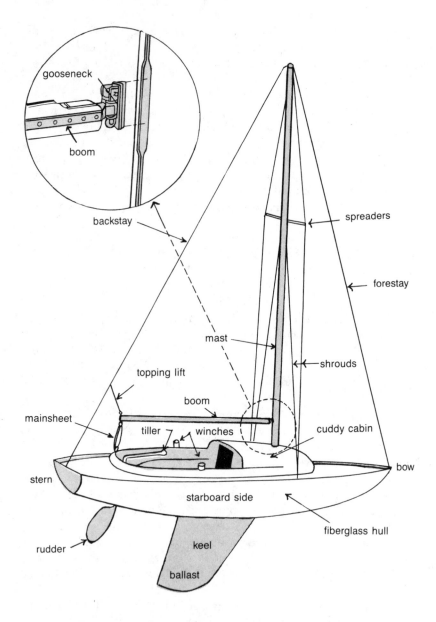

Sailboat nomenclature.

backstay, from the top of the mast to the stern of the boat. The shrouds extend from the top of the mast to the sides of the boat. They're held away from the mast by a pair or more of spreaders which help to make the mast more secure.

We will be using these terms at all times in rigging our boat and on our first few sails. In addition, you must learn the nomenclature of the sail itself, which is basically the same for all three-cornered sails. The foot is the bottom of the sail; the luff is the forward, or leading edge, of the sail; and the leech is the trailing edge of the sail. The three corners of the sail are: the head, which is the top; the tack,

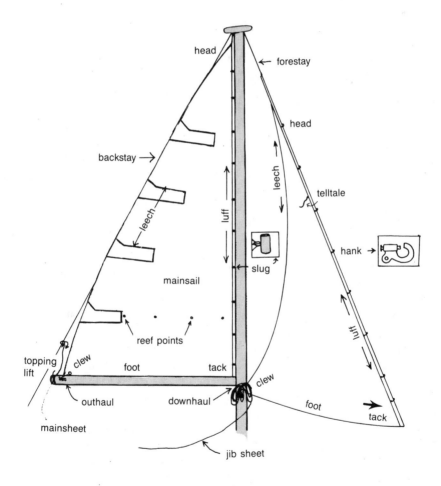

Sail nomenclature.

which is the forward lower corner; and the clew, which is the after, or rearmost corner.

The controlling line is attached to the clew of the sail. In the case of the mainsail, this is a small line called the outhaul. At times, the outhaul is attached permanently to the sail; at other times, the outhaul is attached permanently to the boom. On the jib, there are two controlling lines called jib sheets. Remember, the sheet trims the sail in or eases it out as the course of the boat and the wind direction dictate.

The luff, or leading edge, of the jib is usually attached with a hank of some sort to the forestay of your boat. Many times there is no forestay in small dinghies; the luff itself imparts strength to the mast and acts as a forestay whenever it is up. The luff on your mainsail is attached to the rear of the mast, usually with a sail slide or slug; on smaller boats, a rope along the luff may slide into a groove in the rear of the mast, and the slides will be eliminated.

The mainsail often has reef points, which are small holes or grommets in the sail, parallel to the boom. When sailing in heavy weather, you can reduce the area of the mainsail by passing a line through these reef points, pulling the sail down, and tying it to the boom. The mainsail of most modern boats also has batten pockets into which sticklike battens are inserted to keep the leech of the sail from fluttering and to give better airfoil shape to your sail.

My experience in the sailing school and rental business has taught me that you can tell how well a person knows how to sail by the way he goes about rigging the boat at the dock. Some people study every piece of hardware and fitting, and then rig it all the hard way. I didn't say they do it wrong, but they do it the hard way. Let's all learn to rig the standard conventional boat the correct and easy way.

This may sound funny to an experienced sailor. How do you get aboard to start rigging? A lot can be learned from how a novice approaches this minor problem. A boat without lifelines is no challenge. There are no decisions to make. All we have to do is grasp the standing rigging and step aboard. The boat with lifelines presents a different problem. The solution is to place one foot on the toe rail and grasp the shroud with one hand. You now leave the dock and gracefully swing the dockside foot over the lifeline, followed by the foot on the toe rail, and you're aboard.

I equate this maneuver with the steeplechase. You have the high jump and the water jump. Don't try to do them both at once. Do the water jump first as you put your foot on the toe rail; then complete the high jump by swinging your shoreside leg over the lifeline. These jumps may sound too basic to mention, but if you don't have the basics you will never be able to step aboard properly and gracefully. It sure ruins your day when you do a split on getting aboard – and you and the lunch you were carrying end up on the bottom of the bay.

Safety Equipment

Now that we are aboard, let's proceed to get rigged so we can go sailing. The first thing to check is the safety equipment. Make sure it is all aboard and stowed properly. There are legal requirements and there are sensible requirements. I will give the requirements for a boat from 16 feet to 26 feet as this covers the range of most first-owner boats.

Legal Requirements

1. One Coast Guard–approved life jacket for each person aboard, plus a Type IV device for throwing.
2. One approved fire extinguisher (if there is an engine).
3. One whistle.
4. Distress signals. One set of many acceptable combinations is required.

All equipment must be current and Coast Guard–approved.

Sensible Requirements

Besides all legal requirements, no boat should leave the dock without the following sensible equipment as a bare minimum.

1. Anchor and anchor line.
2. Paddle.
3. Bilge pump.
4. Chart of the area.
5. Compass.

Even before we start to sail we must determine where the wind is coming from. We can rig a boat at any location, but *before* we raise any sail the boat must be pointing *into the wind*.

At a mooring we are fortunate that the boat will always point into the wind – unless there is a very strong current. This is also true when you are at anchor. In a slip or dock other problems develop. In a boat without an engine, you must move your boat to a position where you can moor temporarily with the bow into the wind long enough to raise your sails. A boat with an engine can be powered out of the marina and then slowly turned into the wind as the sails are raised. As more people are sailing and marinas are getting crowded, this last method is coming into universal use. You should always practice rigging and leaving the marina without the use of your engine (if the marina rules don't prevent this); you never know when you may be required to use this skill.

Let's go back to our basic rigging and start with the mainsail. Either sail can be *rigged* first, but the mainsail is always *hoisted* first. As you remove the mainsail from its bag be sure to hold onto the bag. (Sail bags have a nasty habit of blowing overboard.) Tie it to a hand rail or throw it below. We can stow it properly later, but for now we have our hands full of mainsail.

If the sail was put away properly last time, the first corner out of the bag will be the clew. This is the lower rear corner of the sail and the first one we use. The foot, or bottom, of the sail must be attached to the boom by one of three methods. (1) Some sails have just a rope, called a bolt rope, sewn into the foot of the sail. The bolt rope fits into a slot in the boom. Starting at the forward end of the boom, feed the bolt rope into the slot until the clew is out to the end of the boom. This is the only two-man job in rigging; as you pull farther and farther aft, your arms soon become too short to feed in the sail and pull it aft at the same time. If you are alone, it may take you several trips fore and aft before the clew is all the way out to the end of the boom. (2) Mainsails sometimes have sail slugs that are fed into the boom slot. (3) Mainsails sometimes have sail slides that are fed onto an external boom track. For methods 2 and 3 the principle is the same.

Secure the tack, or the forward lower corner, of the sail to the boom where it joins the mast; then secure the outhaul at the end of the boom. There are many different outhaul arrangements, from a simple line that ties the clew to the end of the boom to an internal boom arrangement with blocks or winches arranged to secure the clew. The outhaul does just as its name implies; it hauls the sail out to the end of the boom. There should be enough tension so that the sail does not gap or sag when it is raised, but not so much that it distorts the sail shape and makes wrinkles.

We are now ready to attach the luff, or leading edge, of the sail to the mast. Again we have the option of bolt rope, sail slug, or sail slide. Starting at the tack, or forward lower corner, run your hands along the luff all the way to the head of the sail, the corner that will end up at the top of the mast. This will eliminate any twists in the sail and allow you to start feeding the sail up the mast. If you have slugs or slides, start with the one nearest the head and feed them all onto the mast; then secure them so that they won't slide down. This can be done with anything from a simple line tied around the mast under the last slug or slide to complicated gates and holders built into the mast. If the sail has only a bolt rope, you can start the sail into the mast groove and attach the halyard, the line that raises the sail. Next, cleat the halyard down to hold the sail in position for raising it.

It is now time to insert the battens in the mainsail. There are usually three or four battens, made of wood or fiberglass, that fit into pockets sewn into the trailing edge of the mainsail. The batten helps to keep the proper airfoil shape in the sail by stiffening the trailing edge and giving a smooth curve to the sail. Most battens are tapered. When the thin end is inserted into the batten pocket first, the batten will curve on the forward end to conform with the sail curve; yet it will remain stiff on the trailing edge to give the sail proper shape. Make sure the batten is all the way down in the batten pocket so that it will not come out when the sail is raised.

If there are jiffy reefing lanyards, they should be rigged at this time. But we will save this for the section on reefing and heavy weather sailing. (See part 4.) The mainsail is now ready for hoisting; but before we do that, let's rig the jib. If we raise the mainsail it will only luff, clatter, and perhaps chafe while we rig the jib.

As with the main, first take the jib and remove the bag. Remember to stow the empty bag at once. On the jib we are looking for the tack, or the forward lower corner. You might remember it as the tack because we have to tack it to the deck. There will be some sort of shackle or pin to secure the tack to the bow just aft of the forestay, or jibstay, the wire to which the jib is secured.

After securing the jib tack, we proceed hand over hand up the forward edge of the sail snapping each jib hank in turn on the forestay. Make sure that you snap on all of the hanks in the same direction so that the sail will fit properly. The jib halyard may now be attached to the head of the jib. Again, some sort of shackle is commonly used. Make sure it is completely closed and that the halyard runs free and clear straight to the pulley at the top of the mast. The most common error is wrapping the jib halyard once around the forestay. Check the halyard again.

The jib sheets are next on the program. They will either be permanently attached to the sail or must be attached with some sort of shackle or knot. The bowline is the only knot to use. It has the advantage of forming a permanent loop and still being easy to untie after it has been under a strain. There are various paths for running the sheets back to the cockpit depending on the design of your boat, but these basic rules apply. After the sheets are attached to the clew of the jib, follow hand over hand to the end of one sheet and hold on to the end. Run the sheet back to the block or pulley that is used for this purpose. Sheets normally go over the lifelines, if any, and outside all shrouds to the sheet block and then to the winch.

Try to picture in your mind how this sheet will look when the sail is full and drawing. The sheet must run fair and true without chafing or fouling. Tie a stopper knot in the end of the sheet to prevent it from running out of the block. Repeat the process on the other side of the boat with the other sheet. A figure eight knot is the best stopper knot to use since you can untie it easily after sailing.

Both sails are ready for hoisting, and it is time for one final check. The boat must be pointing into the wind, either under power, at anchor, or tied by the bow to a piling or dock. The boom must be free to swing with the mainsheet loosened and any boom crutch or backstay topping lift ready to be removed. Again make sure that both halyards are attached and running free and clear.

The important point about either raising or lowering your sails is that it should be done smartly – neither at breakneck speed nor as slowly as possibly, but quickly and carefully. A sail that is halfway up or halfway down is a beast over which you have very little control. In order to have everything under control, you must either have your sails all the way up and be ready to depart immediately, or, upon returning, drop them right away and get them secured. If your sails don't go up all the way, look for the reason; don't just haul away until something breaks.

If the boom has a permanently attached gooseneck – the fitting that holds the boom to the mast – you can raise the mainsail at once and adjust the tension on the sail with the halyard. If the boat has a gooseneck that is free to move up and down the mast, be sure the downhaul – the line that hauls the boom and sail down – is loose; raise the sail as high as it will go. After cleating the halyard, adjust the tension on the sail by tightening the downhaul. Make sure the boom crutch or backstay topping lift is removed so that the boom can swing. Now raise the jib. Since jibs don't have downhauls, the tension on the jib is adjusted with the halyard. The loose halyards should be coiled and stowed on the mast.

Now you are ready to sail away. Any adjustments in sail tension will be done after you are sailing and have room to maneuver. Rigging is easy if you do it one step at a time.

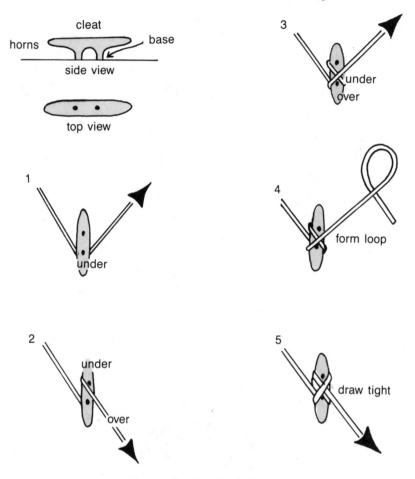

Proper cleating of a halyard.

LEAVING THE DOCK

In leaving the dock, you must always pick a spot which you can sail away from easily after raising your sails. With your boat pointed directly toward the wind and held by a bow line so that it will weather vane in case of a wind shift, you are ready to raise your sails.

We always raise the mainsail first. If the mainsail is raised and the wind shifts, the wind will be blowing on the rearward of the two sails. This will push the stern out of the wind, which will push the bow back into the wind; your sails will luff or flutter like a flag, and you can proceed to raise the next sail. As soon as the mainsail is raised completely, adjust the tension on the sail with either the halyard or the downhaul

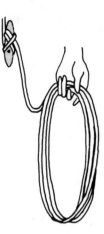 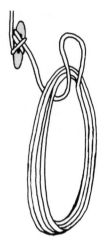 

Hanging the halyard on the cleat

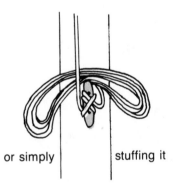

or simply   stuffing it

Two methods of stowing halyards.

so that the sail is tight enough, yet not so tight that it will destroy the airfoil shape built into it by the sailmaker.

When the mainsail is fully raised and luffing, it is time to raise the jib. The jib halyard is hauled on smartly, and the sail is tightened with the halyard—again, tight enough so that the sail is not full of scallops along the leading edge, yet not so tight that you destroy the airfoil shape.

The proper tension on a halyard is difficult for the beginner to determine. It isn't all that important to have it correct immediately. As soon as you fill your sails and are out sailing you'll know whether it's proper or not; you can make an adjustment at that time.

In leaving, we need to have everything stowed properly, our main and jib fully up with the proper tension, and the sheets loose enough so that the sails are luffing. Have someone on the dock cast off the bow line, or go forward yourself and undo the bow line. At this time it is far easier to push the bow sideways so that the wind is no longer coming directly on the bow but rather on the forward third of the boat. Your sails will fill and you can sail away. Later on, as we get further into boat balance, you can learn how to do this same maneuver by backing the jib.

This is an oversimplified explanation of leaving the dock. After we are out and have done more sailing and have studied balance, proper sail trim, and landing, you will find many helpful little things that you can do to make leaving far easier.

REACHING

There are only five things you can do on the water under sail: reaching, running, beating, coming about, and jibing. I told this to a group of sailing school students once and was reminded that I'd forgotten sinking. Sinking is a natural talent and we don't have to teach it to anyone. Let's get on with the first one—reaching.

Reaching—sailing across the wind—is the simplest and easiest point of sailing. We will talk about beam reaching first. When something is off to the side of your boat it is said to be abeam. When you are sailing with the wind on your beam you are beam reaching. This is a very comfortable point of sail as there is a great tolerance for error; you can make mistakes without disaster striking. When an experienced sailor leaves for a pleasant afternoon sail, he will usually, wind and geography permitting, sail away on a beam reach. He knows that, if the wind doesn't shift, he can turn around to come home by beam reaching back on the other side of the wind. In a nutshell, beam reaching is sailing perpendicular to the wind, or crosswind.

How do we adjust our sails for beam reaching? It's easy. Leave them out until they luff, and then trim them in until they stop luffing. Again, in luffing, the sails flutter or shake like a flag. When they stop luffing, stop trimming. Almost all students overtrim. Some students pull on the sheet each time until the sail is board flat; others think that if you trim one foot, two feet must be better. Remember: when in doubt, let them out. When the sail starts to luff, you know it has to

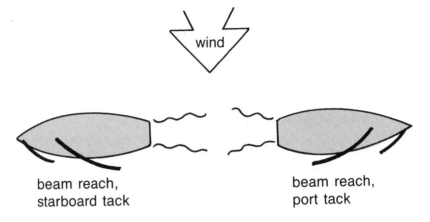

beam reach,   beam reach,
starboard tack   port tack

Reaching is sailing with the wind approximately abeam.

be trimmed; when it stops luffing, you know that you should stop trimming. It's that simple.

Many years ago, when I was just starting in major ocean racing, I was invited to sail the Nassau Cup race on the yacht Doubloon. This race is normally two reaches of about fifteen miles each. In the heat of the start I found myself calling for proper trim on the jib to the winch handlers in the cockpit. After about fifteen minutes of calling trim it dawned on me: I was a guest on the boat sailing with near pros for the first time, and I had the effrontery to be telling them how to trim. I tried to get relieved and do something less demanding, but the captain wouldn't let me. After the race was over, I cornered him and, since I felt I could learn a lot, asked him to tell me how he trimmed his sails. Assuring me that I had done fine, he said that all you have to do is *leave the sails out until they luff and trim them in until they stop luffing*—one of sailing's great truths. As an aside, we did well enough in the final race to win the SORC fleet championship.

Let's review. Beam reaching is sailing with the wind abeam, letting your sails out until they luff, and trimming them in until they stop. You always trim the sail that is farthest forward first. Start with the jib and then trim the main since the wind spilled out of the jib will affect the main. Close reaching is sailing closer into the wind so that the wind is forward of the beam. Broad reaching is sailing farther out of the wind so that the wind is abaft, or behind the beam. Having seen many boats overtrimmed, I can't stress this one point enough: let the sails out until they luff and then trim them in until they stop luffing.

If you want to start a good argument someday, get ten sailors together and try to fix the exact point where beam reaching ends and close or broad reaching starts. I don't think it matters; they just blend into each other and all are handled basically the same way.

As we reach off toward the horizon we will have to turn and head back home. One way to do this is to "come about," or "tack."

COMING ABOUT

Coming about, or tacking, is the maneuver in which you change course by bringing the bow of the boat or the leading edge of the sail into and through the wind to fill the sails on the opposite side of the boat. This is a very simple definition of one of the most complex maneuvers you will do on a sailboat. Let's go further: When a boat is sailing with the wind over the starboard, or right-hand side, of the boat and the sails are filled on the port, or left-hand side, of the boat, the boat is said to be on the starboard tack. Wind from starboard equals starboard tack. Conversely, wind from the port side equals port tack.

This is all fine. But what happens when you are running and the wind is from astern, or behind you? You are on the tack opposite of the side the main boom is trimmed on. If the main boom is to port you are on starboard tack, and vice versa for port tack. A boat sailing on a beam reach on the port tack with the wind coming from the left side will come about by turning into and through the wind. The wind will fill the sails on the starboard side, and the boat will sail on a reverse course. This completes a 180-degree turn. Of course, you do not always have to turn 180 degrees; you can make any degree of turn you wish, but you must go through the wind far enough to fill your sails on the other side of the wind.

Many beginners have trouble learning to steer with a tiller. Here are a couple of tips to help you steer better. Remember, we want to go into the wind. To go into the wind put the tiller into the sail. To come out of the wind bring the tiller out of the sail. It works. Try it. People who still have trouble with the tiller should try to imagine that the hand that is holding the tiller is holding onto the bottom center of their auto steering wheel. If you move your hand to the right, the boat or car will move to the left; if you move your hand to the left, the car or boat will move to the right. Again I say, try it. It works.

We are now ready to start our coming-about maneuver. Commands should be used. The helmsman or skipper, whoever's in charge, should command, "Ready about" or "Prepare to come about" or any other easily understood command. When the crew answers "Ready," the skip-

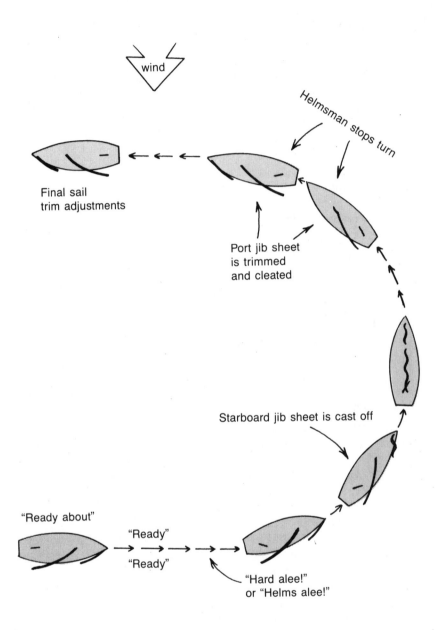

wind

Helmsman stops turn

Final sail
trim adjustments

Port jib sheet
is trimmed
and cleated

Starboard jib sheet is cast off

"Ready about"

"Ready"

"Ready"

"Hard alee!"
or "Helms alee!"

Coming about from a reach to a reach.

per again commands, "Hard alee" or "Helms alee" or simply "Come about," and the maneuver starts.

At the command of "Ready about," the crew on the jib sheets should uncleat the leeward, or working jib, sheet. They should make sure the jib sheet is still on the winch and properly trimmed since we need all of the drive out of the sails we can get. The crew should prepare the windward, or lazy jib, sheet for trimming by taking one or two turns around the jib sheet winch.

At this point, the answer, "Ready," is given by the crew to the captain. It is also nice to notify the cook of your intentions in time for him to prevent the prime rib from ending up on the floor. Most cooks have sharp ears and are ready in any case. If you are having only peanut butter and jelly don't bother warning the cook. A little bilge water will never hurt your sandwiches. After receiving the "Ready" answer, the skipper gives the "Helms alee" command, and the helmsman starts turning the boat.

When the boat has turned far enough into the wind for the jib to luff, the working, or leeward, sheet is thrown off. Do not, I repeat, do not loosen the sheet until the sail starts to luff. Loosening the sheet when the sail is still drawing is like turning off your engine. As the boat continues its turn, the jib will work its way over to the other side of the boat. What started as the lazy sheet now becomes the working sheet. It is trimmed in and cleated.

Under no circumstances try to pull the jib across with the sheet. This would cause the jib to fill from the wrong side. A jib filled on the wrong side is a "backed" jib, and it's difficult, if not impossible, to come about. Don't trim the jib until the wind has brought it to the proper side of the boat. Trying to pull the jib across and causing it to back, and releasing the jib sheet too early in the turn are common mistakes of beginning jib handlers.

While the jib handlers are doing their job, the helmsman at the tiller must do his. A boat will not sail straight when you release the tiller the way a car will drive straight when you release the wheel. The helmsman must make an effort to compensate for the turning momentum of the boat. You must start to correct before you arrive at your new course. This will become part of your normal steering procedure with a little practice. For now, be aware of the necessity of compensating to prevent overturning.

When the boat is on its new course, final sail trim adjustments should be made, starting with the jib. You may have noticed that there has been no mention of what to do with the mainsail while coming

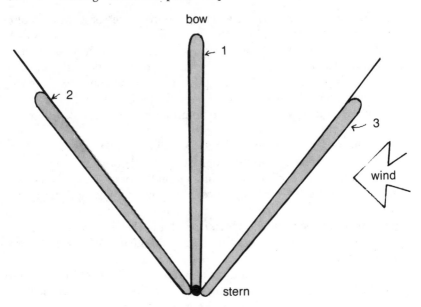

Tiller position in coming about.
Tiller position 1. Tiller in center and boat on a straight course. *Tiller position 2.* Tiller moved to leeward to start the boat coming about. *Tiller position 3.* Tiller moved to position 3 momentarily to stop the turning of the boat and almost immediately returned to position 1 to sail a straight course.

about. In basic sailing there is little, if anything, to do with the mainsail until you arrive at the final course and make the last trim adjustments. Remember: let the sails out until they luff and then trim them in until they stop luffing. When they stop luffing, stop trimming.

We have discussed coming about from a reach to a reach, but of course you can come about from any point of sailing to any other point of sailing.

RETURNING TO THE DOCK

In returning to the dock, remember there are only two ways to stop a sailboat: one is to point it directly into the wind so that all your sails luff and you coast to a stop with the dock or the mooring buoy directly in front of you, close enough so that you can tie up; the other is to hit something. I'm sure that with your own boat you would far prefer to come up and coast to a gentle stop. The most important thing in shooting a landing is making sure you have an escape route planned. If you have a margin for error built into your maneuver, you can easily remove yourself from trouble.

It is wise to practice bringing the boat through half a come about directly up into the wind, letting your sails luff, and seeing how far your boat will coast, or "headreach," into the wind before it comes to a complete stop. Without this information, it is difficult to make a proper landing. A good rule of thumb is that the heavier the boat, the farther it will headreach, or coast, directly into the wind before coming to a stop. There's another factor to take into consideration: the faster the wind is blowing, usually the shorter the distance it will take you to coast to a stop. This happens because the wind blows on your sails harder as you are heading directly into the wind and offers a more effective break.

Never drop your sails before you reach your mooring or dock. If you do, it's as if you were throwing your engine overboard in a powerboat; you'll have no way to propel yourself out of trouble should it arise. You must remember that the wind is constantly changing direction slightly, and that is why you need full control of your boat until you have it tied by the bow. Then you can take the sails down. As soon as you are tied up, drop your jib sail first; the mainsail will continue to act as a weather vane to hold your boat pointed directly into the wind. When the jib is on deck, get your mainsail down and secured.

Many beginning students hold the boom with one hand as it swings back and forth over their heads when they're heading into the wind. This is an extremely poor practice; it can cause your sails to fill with wind and send you sailing off in the wrong direction. Do not hold the boom or tighten the sheets until the sail has been lowered. You will notice in the docking diagram in part 2 that there are many places — with varying degrees of safety and difficulty — to bring the boat in under sail. As we move further into our instruction, we will encounter far more complicated docking situations.

You have now completed part 1 in learning to sail "The Annapolis Way." You have only the barest, most basic facts of getting your boat away from the dock, sailing on a reach, coming about, sailing back to the dock, and making a landing. Please complete the checklist and exercise immediately following part 1 before you venture out on your first trip away from the dock. We strongly suggest that you do this only in the most sheltered inland waters on the nicest of days and that you be accompanied by an experienced sailor or sailing instructor if one's available. If no better helper is available, I would advise you to go out with somebody who has at least studied this portion of the manual.

RIGGING CHECKLIST

Safety Check
__ One life vest per person
__ One throwable flotation device, easily accessible
__ One anchor and line
__ One paddle
__ One bucket or pump

Rigging Mainsail
__ Bow is into the wind
__ Open bag and remove sails
__ Stow bag
__ Locate mainsail
__ Locate clew
__ Locate slot or track on boom
__ Feed bolt rope or slides on foot of sail onto boom
__ Pull clew of sail to end of boom
__ Secure tack of sail to tack fitting on boom
__ Connect clew to end of boom with outhaul
__ Tighten and secure outhaul
__ Uncleat mainsheet
__ Pull several feet of slack through mainsheet blocks
__ Locate luff of sail
__ Slide hands up luff to head of sail (this removes twists)
__ Secure luff of sail to mast using either slides, slugs, or luff rope
__ Secure slides or slugs with pin
__ Locate main halyard (starboard side of mast)
__ Uncleat and clear main halyard
__ Secure halyard to head of sail

Rigging Jib
__ Take jib onto foredeck
__ Locate tack of jib
__ Locate tack fitting on bow of boat
__ Secure tack of jib to fitting
__ Locate luff wire or rope sewn in front edge of jib
__ Locate bottom jib stay hank (snap hook) fastened to luff
__ Locate forestay
__ Attach hank to forestay
__ Attach remaining hanks, in sequence, to stay – all hanks facing same
direction

__ Locate jib sheets and attach to clew of jib
__ Separate sheets
__ Lead one sheet aft on either side of boat, usually outside shrouds
__ Lead sheets through fairlead blocks on deck to cockpit area
__ Tie stopper knot in the bitter end of sheet; be sure to set stopper knot
__ Locate jib halyard (port side)
__ Uncleat and clear jib halyard
__ Attach halyard to head of jib

Hoisting Main
__ Hoist mainsail by pulling on halyard
__ Hoist sail all the way up to proper tension if fixed gooseneck
__ Secure halyard to cleat
__ Coil and stow halyard
__ Pull down on downhaul until luff has desired tension if boat is equipped with sliding gooseneck
__ Secure downhaul
__ Release topping lift or remove boom crutch if it interferes with boom movement

Double Check
__ Is boom free to swing?
__ Is sail luffing?

Hoisting Jib
__ Hoist jib by pulling on halyard
__ Put proper tension on the luff by tightening the halyard
__ Coil and stow the halyard

Double Check
__ Both sails luffing
__ All sheets free
__ All loose gear securely stowed

GOOD SAILING!

REVIEW QUESTIONS
(Answers follow part 7)

   1. What three things are needed to make a boat sail into the wind?
   2. What are the three common types of centerboards?

3. Where should the swing keel be positioned when sailing down-wind?
4. What are the two chief functions of the keel?
5. What is the difference between a sheet and a sail?
6. What legal sea safety equipment is required on a sailboat of between 16 and 26 feet?
7. Which sail is always hoisted first when rigging the boat?
8. Which end of the batten goes forward in the mainsail?
9. Name the corner of the jib that is attached to the boat first.
10. What is the best knot to tie in the cockpit end of your jib sheet?
11. What is the most important thing to check before raising your sail?
12. Where is the wind coming from when you are reaching?
13. Complete this statement about sail trim: When in doubt _____ _____ _____.
14. Do we turn the bow of the boat into or out of the wind to come about?
15. To go into the wind, do you move the tiller into or out of the sail?
16. What is the only practical way to stop a sailboat?

SAILING EXERCISE I

On your first practice trip follow the rigging checklist closely to raise your sails properly. Drop your sails, stow them away, and rig your boat again. You want this to become so routine that it is automatic.

Now you should leave the dock and practice beam reaching and coming about for about an hour. Try to sail a straight course while keeping the wind at right angles to your boat's course.

This is the part where you need three eyes: one to watch your course; one to watch the telltales in order to check wind direction; and one to check the sails for the proper trim. Try not to overcorrect. Make only small tiller corrections so that you will not sail a scalloped course. Don't overdo it. Return to the dock and put your boat away.

If you wish, start at the beginning and do it all over again. Don't forget, don't go out on any but the nicest day and have with you an instructor, an experienced sailor, or someone who has at least studied this section.

Good luck and good sailing.

Sailing Maneuvers

BEATING

The next point of sailing we will cover is beating – sailing as close into the wind as you can without luffing, yet maintaining good boat speed. No boat can sail directly into the wind. You can, however, sail to a point that is directly into the wind – or to windward – by sailing first on one side of the wind and then coming about into and through the wind so that the wind fills your sails from the other side. In this way, you can sail even closer to your objective.

Through a series of tacks and come abouts you will sail to a point that is to windward. Let's go back to square one. We want to sail to a point directly into the wind; but when we steer the boat in that direction the sails luff. Remember I said to let the sails out until they luff and then trim them in until they don't. Now, we trim the sails in as flat as they can go and the sails *still* luff since we are pointing directly into the wind. We must stop the sails from luffing. The only way to do that is to turn the boat – *and with it the sails* – out of the wind until the luffing stops, and then stop turning. You now have the sails properly trimmed and your course established to sail as close into the wind

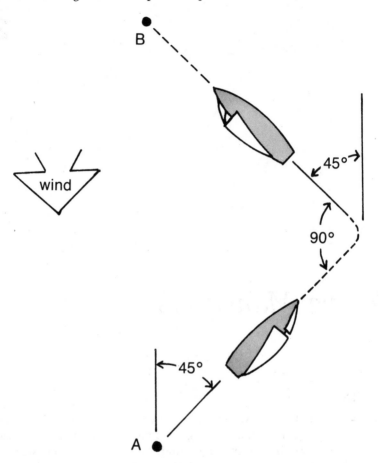

This maneuver is called beating, beating to windward, or if repeated quickly, short tacking.

as possible. You will find that your course is approximately 45 degrees out of the wind.

If you continue to sail on that course until your destination is abeam, and then come about into and through the wind until your sails fill on the other side of the wind, you will find that you have made a 90-degree turn and are now heading for your objective. We turned 45 degrees directly into the wind and then 45 degrees more until our sails filled on the other side of the wind.

I lied to you earlier when I said that, in beating, the sails are trimmed in as flat as they will go. A strong crew may trim the sails so flat that they destroy the airfoil shape. This will kill boat speed. Conversely, if you don't trim the sails flat enough, you will not be able to sail close into the wind without luffing and will have to sail a longer course. Your boat is different than all others; a little practice will teach you just how close into the wind you can sail for maximum performance. Keep in mind that in beating to windward we first trim our sails in as flat as they will go without destroying the airfoil shape; we then steer as close into the wind as we can without luffing.

When you are sailing as close into the wind as you can on one tack, which is approximately a 45-degree angle to the wind, and you come about into and through the wind to sail on the other side of the wind at about 45 degrees – and if you repeat this maneuver frequently – you are short tacking. I don't like the word tacking. It has too many definitions. You are on a tack, either port or starboard, any time you are sailing. You come about by heading into and through the wind until your sails fill on the new tack. Yet, today you will be understood if you say, "Let's tack." What you have said is, "Let's change tacks by coming about." I feel that by using the term "Let's come about" you are a little clearer in your intentions than by using "Let's tack" when you are already on a tack.

RUNNING

Running is sailing downwind with the wind behind you and the sails well out. There's some dissension as to where broad reaching ends and running starts. It doesn't really matter since they blend into one another. My statement about letting the sails out until they luff still holds water. If the wind is aft, or from behind, you can leave the mainsail all the way out until the boom is touching the shrouds – the wires that support the mast. Since the sail won't luff, we know that we can't let it out any more and that it must be in the right place. In effect, we have the sail at right angles to the wind to get the maximum area exposed to the wind for the maximum push.

The jib is very difficult to keep full of wind at this time because it is in the wind shadow of the mainsail. If you pull the jib over to the other side of the boat out of the mainsail's wind shadow, the jib will fill with wind. You can then sail downwind wing and wing – that is, sailing with one sail on each side of the boat.

A whisker pole is often used at this point to help keep the jib full of wind. The whisker pole is rigged from the clew of the jib to a fitting on the mast. It is perpendicular to both the centerline of the boat and the wind and holds the jib out to catch the wind better.

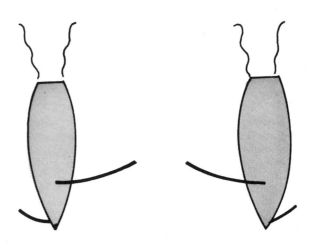

Left, **Running wing and wing, starboard tack;** *right*, **running wing and wing, port tack.**

Many advanced sailors will fly their multicolored spinakers while running to put up maximum sail for maximum speed. For now, let's learn to use our basic sails properly before going on to more sophisticated rigs.

JIBING

Let's go on to the great bugaboo—jibing. First, a simple definition: jibing is changing tacks by moving the stern of the boat and the trailing edge of the sail into and through the wind. Jibing has had so many bad things written about it in the past that I have had students turn white at the mere mention of the word and freeze at the tiller in its execution. Accidental jibing in high winds is dangerous. Intentional jibing in average conditions is about as adventuresome as picking strawberries. It is all in being prepared and doing it right.

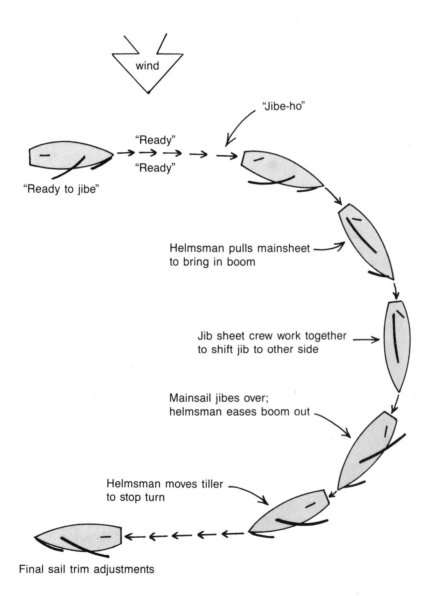

wind

"Jibe-ho"

"Ready"

"Ready"

"Ready to jibe"

Helmsman pulls mainsheet
to bring in boom

Jib sheet crew work together
to shift jib to other side

Mainsail jibes over;
helmsman eases boom out

Helmsman moves tiller
to stop turn

Final sail trim adjustments

Jibing from a reach to a reach.

Why would anyone choose jibing to change tacks when he could change tacks by coming about? It is as simple as what way do we want to go. If coming about will take you closer to your destination, come about. If jibing will take you closer to your goal, jibe.

I was once asked, "If you were on a beam reach on a nice day in open water and you wanted to turn 180 degrees by either jibing or coming about, which would you do, and why?" I answered at once that I would come about since that is easier. I equate coming about and jibing with making right or left turns in a car. Right is easier because of traffic; coming about is easier because of sail handling.

Remember that we hardly mentioned the mainsail in coming about? Well, it is the most important thing in a jibe. When you turn into the wind, the sails, being fastened at the leading edge, slowly start to luff and then slowly fill on the other side. When you turn out of the wind or jibe, the sails are all full on one side; as the wind gets on the far side of them, they suddenly fill and are sometimes thrown quite violently to the other side of the boat. It is this violence we must eliminate to have a successful jibe.

Both the mainsail and the jib need careful handling, but let's start with the mainsail. Commands should be used. The helmsman or skipper sings out, "Ready to jibe," or "Prepare to jibe"; when the crew is prepared they answer, "Ready." The crew gets ready by preparing the jib sheets as in coming about, and, in addition, by uncleating the main sheet but not letting it run out.

When the skipper gives the command, "Jibe-ho," or simply "Jibing," the helmsman starts his turn out of the wind. Remember, the tiller moves out of the sail. This is the critical point. The mainsheet must be trimmed in rapidly for two reasons: (1) If the sheet and sail are trimmed in flat, when the sail fills on the other side there is no slack in the sheet allowing the sail to pick up momentum and slam from side to side; (2) If the sheet is trimmed in, it is also holding the boom down, preventing all kinds of bad things I won't go into here.

Remember, we trim the main in and down and let it out rapidly as the jibe is completed. Many people will reach back and pull all of the sheets at once with one hand and then release them as the boom swings over. This is all right in light winds, but I have seen a sail fill and yank a person right out of the cockpit. I have also seen very nasty rope burns where the mainsheet slipped through a person's hands. I've had both of the above accidents happen to me. I guess we all learn by making mistakes; I just hope I can help you make only little ones.

While the boat is turning we must pay attention to the jib. As the trailing edge of the jib passes through the wind, the jib trimmers must work as a team. They must keep a slight tension on both sheets and work the sail across the foredeck by loosening one sheet as the other is pulled in. If they don't keep enough tension on the sheets, the jib has a tendency to fly forward and wrap itself around the forestay. Keeping too much tension on the jib sheets is better than not enough. If too much tension is maintained, all that will happen is the jib will back. A backed jib can be cured quickly by trimming the proper sheet when the jibe is completed.

As in coming about, the helmsman must make a smooth turn and make his correction to stop turning before arriving at the final course. But the turn in jibing is out of the wind.

I have explained the jibe maneuver as if there were four people aboard the boat—the helmsman, two jib sheet trimmers, and a mainsheet trimmer. More often than not there will be only two—the helmsman, who will handle the mainsheet, and one crew member, who will handle the jib sheets. If the boat is to be manned by one person, we must set up priorities; no one can do all of the required things at once.

In coming about, forget about the main; focus your full attention on the jib sheets and the tiller until the maneuver is complete. In jibing, take up the slack in the lazy jib sheet and then concentrate on the main and tiller until the maneuver is complete. Then you have time to trim the jib properly. This may not look good, but it sure is safe.

You now know everything there is to know about sailing. Any time you are sailing, you are either reaching, running, beating, jibing, or coming about. From now on, we're going to learn combinations of these to make a real sailor out of you and to make sailing easier and safer.

RETURNING TO THE DOCK

If you recall our discussion in part 1 about docking, we approach the dock on a reach, turn the boat directly into the wind, and coast to a stop. This is nothing more than reaching and half of a come about, as it were, turning the boat directly into the wind and coasting, or head-reaching, to a stop. There are many other ways you can approach moorings and docks. The easiest, of course, is what we've just discussed: approaching the dock on a reach, turning into the wind, and coasting in to a stop.

Sometimes, however, there will be a situation where the approach to the dock must be made from windward. You then have to come dead downwind to the dock and land on the face where the wind blows you

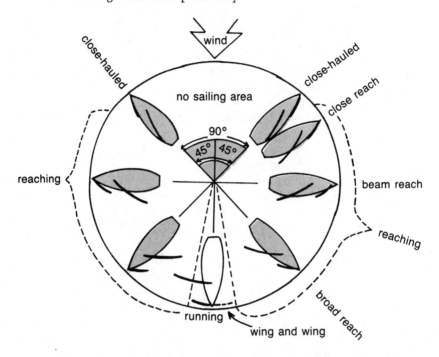

Point of sail. There are three principal points of sail: close-hauled, reaching, and running. They are not three precise courses relative to the wind but rather approximate courses. Here, a close-hauled boat is being sailed as close to the wind as possible without luffing the sails. A running boat has the wind directly aft or astern. Between the two is a large area broadly termed reaching. However, reaching is generally further refined into close reaching, beam reaching, and broad reaching. There are no precise boundaries between these points of sail.

directly onto the dock. In this case you have no opportunity to head up into the wind and headreach to a stop at the dock ahead of you.

There are two ways this maneuver can be accomplished. The first way is to head downwind directly into the dock and, by either jibing or coming about, turn the boat around 180 degrees and point directly into the wind – and remember, coming about is easier than jibing. When you have the boat pointed directly into the wind, it will coast to a stop. You can then drop your sails and drift back onto the dock. This sounds very easy, but you'd better have your paddle ready to make a few strokes to straighten out the boat in order to drift back properly onto the face of the dock. The difficulty with this maneuver is getting away from the dock again when you want to leave.

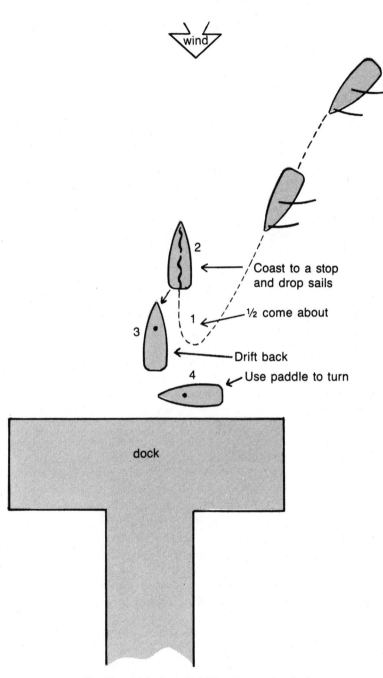

wind

2

Coast to a stop
and drop sails

1 — ½ come about

3

Drift back

4 Use paddle to turn

dock

Docking with the wind blowing on the dock.

The second solution is more reasonable. If the boat traffic will permit, approach the dock downwind, turn directly up into the wind, coast to a stop, and drop an anchor. Drift back on your anchor line, drop your sail, and hold yourself off the dock with the anchor while you secure everything properly. Then you can drift back onto the dock, tie up, and release your anchor line so that it is slack. That way the local powerboat jockey won't whiz by and cut it in two. You can enjoy your stay ashore, and when you're ready to leave, just tighten up on your anchor line and release your dock line. You'll have the boat pointing directly into the wind, allowing you to raise your sails. Pull yourself forward on the anchor line, raise the anchor, and sail away with no problems.

People do not use anchors enough. They are valuable tools on board. Take, for example, a situation where you're sailing a small boat onto the beach with the wind behind you. In this case, that beach is called a lee shore because the wind is blowing the boat onto shore and the shore is to your lee, or leeward of you. Rather than run the boat right up onto the beach at the risk of your rudder and centerboard, head up into the wind, drop anchor, and drift back onto the beach, slowly paying out the anchor line.

Catamarans, especially the ones that do not have centerboards, can sail right onto the beach with no regard for damage to the boat. In centerboard or keel boats, however, it is impossible. You must turn up into the wind, drop your anchor, and ease the boat back by hand. Remember, never sail into anyplace where you do not have a means of escape and a plan for leaving.

It is extremely dangerous to sail into a cul-de-sac where there is no way out under easy sail. However, there will be times when your boat is windbound – that is, when the wind is holding you against the dock or in the slip. The only way of getting out of that situation is with some kind of power assistance. You can use either engine power or what the oldtime sailors called "white-ash breeze". White ash is a choice material for making paddles. You can either motor away or paddle using "Swedish steam," which is just muscles, to where you can point the bow into the wind and raise the sails.

Sailing off a beach against the wind on a small centerboard boat can be a real problem. You can't beat to windward because you must have the centerboard down or you'll slip sideways. And you can't put the centerboard down because you're not in deep enough water.

You have to get the boat out into deeper water. The best way to do that is to carry the anchor out as far as you can wade, set the anchor on the bottom, and string the anchor line back to shore. Rig the boat

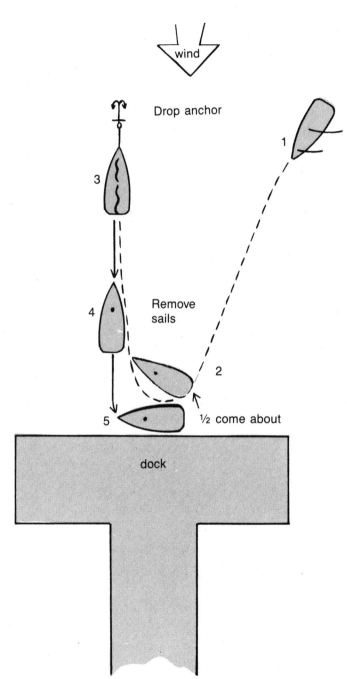

wind

Drop anchor

3

Remove
sails

4

2

5

½ come about

dock

Using your anchor for better control when docking with the wind on the dock.

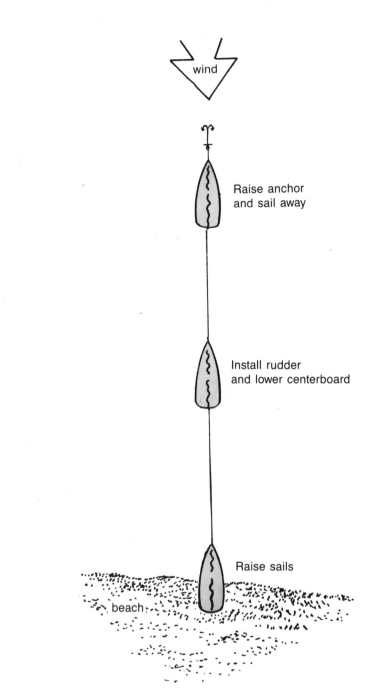

Using your anchor to help you sail away from a lee shore.

completely while it is on the beach, get your sails up, and get everything ready to go.

Launch the boat and pull it out on the anchor line. It will weather vane and point directly into the wind. Climb into the boat and pull yourself forward into water deep enough to lower the centerboard. Push the rudder down or mount the rudder and lower the centerboard. Then if you pull yourself forward rapidly, you will even get steerage way – the speed it takes to have the water passing over the rudder fast enough in order to steer. Just as there must be wind passing over the sails in order for the boat to move, there must also be water passing over the rudder to allow you to steer. Raise the anchor, and you're underway and in complete control. I certainly do not recommend this maneuver in any surf unless you are extremely experienced.

Many times, if you are going to return to the same location after your day's sail, it behooves you to tie a fender to the end of the anchor line; leave your anchor on the bottom with the fender as a buoy to give yourself a safe place to return on this hostile lee shore. Leaving moorings, docks, and beaches and returning to them is probably one of the most difficult points of sailing. There are two reasons for this: one, you have obstacles near at hand; and two, you have people there to criticize you if you do something wrong. If you're out in the middle of the bay and you make a mistake, nobody sees you; it really doesn't matter much as long as it's not fatal.

On shore, there's always somebody giving you advice. Most novice sailors take shortcuts. *Do not take shortcuts.* You must go through the whole series of checklists. You may be a little slower than the next guy, but you're going to be right each time you go out.

At this point, you're ready to do some more complicated maneuvering under sail. Again, I strongly recommend that you have a qualified sailor or instructor with you and that you do not go out in wind any stronger than we recommended after the first section. Leave your mooring or dock as you did before, proceed out into the open water – again, making sure you're in a sheltered area with light winds – and practice reaching and coming about as you did in part 1.

After you've come about several times, try a nice reach and then jibe to the other tack. Then try running downwind wing and wing, with the main trimmed to one side and the jib to the other. At the end of your run, you will be forced to beat back to your starting point; the only way to get back from being downwind is to beat back into it with a series of tacks and come abouts.

After a few hours of practice on running, reaching, beating, jibing, and coming about, you'll return to the dock, beach, or mooring and

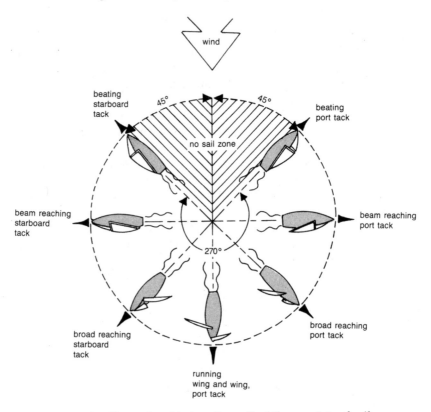

You should now be able to sail on all of these points of sail.

prepare for part 3. You should complete your checklist and the exercise on part 2 before going out.

REVIEW QUESTIONS
(Answers follow part 7)

1. In beating to windward should you trim your sails as flat as possible?
2. What three things must you watch at all times while beating to windward?
3. What is short tacking?
4. What can we use to help hold the jib out when we are running downwind?
5. What is it called when you are sailing downwind with the mainsail on one side of the boat and the jib on the other?

6. Do we put the bow or the stern into and through the wind when jibing?
7. Which sail is more important to control when jibing?
8. How can we keep our boat off the beach or dock when we come into land with the wind blowing onshore?
9. What is necessary for steerage way?
10. Should you ever sail into a cul-de-sac?

SAILING EXERCISE II

Follow the checklist from part 1 and rig your boat. Make sure you don't raise your sails until you are pointing directly into the wind.

Review Sailing Exercise I by sailing on a nice reach and coming about a few times. Now you can practice jibing from a beam reach to a beam reach. Make sure you are controlling the mainsail when jibing. Go onto a run and try sailing downwind wing and wing. Don't be disappointed if you can't keep the jib full of air at all times.

Be careful of the accidental jibe. Turn back upwind and beat back to your starting point through a series of tacks and come abouts.

Sail downwind once more, wing and wing, and beat back again. Keep this up until you find that you are comfortable and capable. Return to the beach or dock.

3

Safe Sailing

MAN OVERBOARD

The most frightening sound at sea is the cry, "Man overboard!" The first, and most important, task is to throw something that floats to the man in the water. By law, a throwable device must at all times be easily accessible in the cockpit of the boat. Get it overboard to the man as soon as possible, but don't stop there. Throw everything in the cockpit overboard to the man: boat cushions, spare jackets, spare life rings. Iceboxes made of styrofoam float beautifully. The larger the slick of floating debris you create on the ocean, the easier it will be to find the man.

A bobbing head in any type of chop is very difficult to see. Larger boats should be equipped like racing boats with a combination of man-overboard light, life ring, drogue, man-overboard flag, water light, and whistle. This may seem like a lot of gear, but it really isn't much. And you'll really appreciate it if you're the one who happens to go overboard. The large flag is easy for the man in the water to see; it is also an easy point of reference for the people on the boat.

Somebody left on the boat should take the sole responsibility of keeping the man in view; he should do nothing with manning the ship. While scurrying around the boat to get the best possible view, he should point his finger at the man at all times so that he will not lose sight of him.

Once the cry, "Man overboard," goes out, the helmsman immediately puts the boat onto a reach. It really doesn't matter whether it's port or starboard tack, but get the boat sailing on a course that is perpendicular to the wind. Sail away from the man with the wind directly abeam, jibe to put yourself slightly downwind of where the man went in, and sail back with the wind directly abeam. Theoretically, you'll return to the original spot and find your man overboard waiting for you. Don't jibe too fast too soon after the cry, "Man overboard." If you do, you'll only go around in circles, close to the man overboard but never far enough away to give yourself maneuvering room to get up to him. Better to wait ten, fifteen, or even twenty seconds and do the maneuver properly; give yourself room and control to sail up to your man. It will usually take you that long to clear your wits.

Sail to a point that is two or three boat lengths downwind of the victim. This is an arbitrary figure, but you have to practice with your boat to find out how far it will headreach or coast into the wind. You should be far enough away from the man so that when you are directly downwind, you can make your half come about directly into the wind. Coast to a stop with the man directly alongside the area of the cockpit where you are able to help him. Of course, you can't be much help to him if you run him over. Apart from this caution, you'll notice how similar this maneuver is to approaching moorings and docks.

As you learn how the boat headreaches, you will be able to perform this maneuver with great satisfaction. Have a line with a large bowline tied into it ready to slip over the man and under his arms; if the wind shifts and the sails fill causing you to start sailing away from him, he won't have to rely on his grip, or you on yours, to keep him alongside the boat. Bring the line in close and attach him to the boat as quickly as possible. Keep a swimming or boarding ladder ready if you have one; if the man overboard is able to move on his own power, this is by far the simplest way of getting him aboard. I like the permanently installed boarding ladders on the transom of most vessels of about twenty feet or longer. Not only are they great for recreation, but they are also an important safety feature.

If the man is unable to get onto the boat unassisted, perhaps you can attach the line that you have run under his arms to the main halyard, lift him with the main halyard winch, and hoist him aboard. Or,

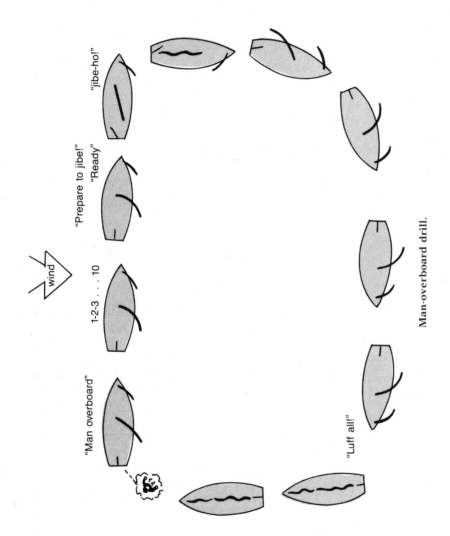

"jibe-ho!"

"Prepare to jibe!"
"Ready"

wind

1-2-3 . . . 10

"Man overboard"

Man-overboard drill.

"Luff all!"

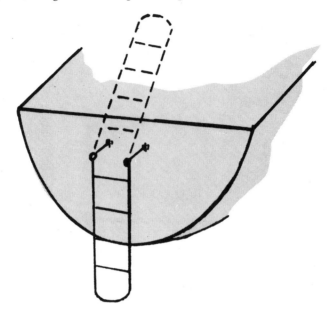

A permanent boarding ladder (shown in raised and lowered positions) is a helpful safety device on large boats.

leaving the block attached to the boom, you can disconnect the end of the mainsheet from the vessel; then move the boom out over the water, use the block and tackle of the mainsheet to hoist the man up, and swing him in with the boom.

Another method: If the man is unable to get aboard under his own power, try dropping the mainsail overboard; leave it attached to the boom and to the halyard, but disconnect it completely from the mast. You can float the victim in the hammocklike pocket formed by the sail in the water. As the halyard is hoisted, the man will be lifted out of the water in the belly of the sail and you can roll him on the deck "Spanish windlass"-style. If the man is injured and unable to get on-board the boat by himself, he'll probably need help getting into the belly of the sail.

The purpose of the man-overboard maneuver is to get your man out of the water. Let's save putting other men in the water as a last resort.

Once I lost a very obese person overboard from a small boat and wasn't able to get him back aboard. I simply lashed him — tied him so

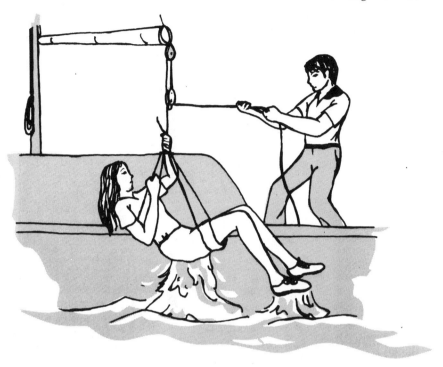

Hoisting a person aboard using the mainsheet. If you don't know how to tie a bowline on a bite, a single bowline under the person's arms will work.

that he could hang onto the side of the boat – got a life jacket under him, and sailed the boat back to shallow water where he could walk ashore.

Remember, man overboard always happens when you are least expecting it and least prepared for it. Every situation is different – the size of the boat, the number of crew left on board, the condition of the person in the water, the velocity of the wind, the size of the waves, the distance from shore. These are all factors that the prudent skipper must quickly weigh in his mind in order to use all of his seamanship skills to get that person back aboard.

Somebody once told me that it really doesn't matter whether you know man-overboard drills or not. I couldn't understand that statement until he went on to say that what really matters is whether or not the person you're sailing with knows man-overboard drills. Think about that; it's true. If you're in the water and the person who's in the boat doesn't know man-overboard drills, it doesn't matter how good *you* are.

hoist on halyard

sail

Using the sail Spanish windlass–style to bring a man aboard.

Let's hope you teach the other guy proper man-overboard procedures. The wife who says she only wants to know enough about sailing to help her husband could really help if she knew enough to go back and pick him up. So, do learn and practice man-overboard drills.

TRIMMING FOR SPEED

All we have talked about in sail trim so far is: when in doubt, let it out. Let a sail out until it luffs; trim it in until it stops luffing. When the sail stops luffing, stop trimming; the sail's trimmed. This is very basic, but it doesn't cover the little, and the not-so-little, adjustments that make a properly trimmed sail. Let's start with our jibs.

The Jib

The most common error in trimming a jib is not actually a mistake in trimming at all; it is an error in putting the jib up. If the halyard is not drawn tight enough, there will be a scallop at every hank going up the luff—the leading edge of the sail—which almost completely destroys the airfoil shape. Remember, we need that airfoil shape to get the boat moving properly. Conversely, make sure your jib doesn't go up so tight that you destroy its airfoil shape.

If there are heavy winds, the jib has to go up almost as tight as you can make it. Larger boats will have a jib winch to assist in this function. On smaller boats, you can get the jib up tight by "sweating it up." To sweat the jib up, place the halyard under the cleat, grab the halyard between the cleat and the top of the mast, and pull out on it very hard to create slack. Then take in the slack on the end of the halyard with your other hand. Quickly, without releasing the tension on the halyard, cleat it down. Normally, this will get the jib on a small boat up as tight as you want it to be.

The next major fault in trimming is having the jib fairleads improperly set. The jib sheets lead from the clew of the jib back to a block, or fairlead, located on the deck, and onto your cockpit winch or some other mechanical device that holds the sheet in the cockpit. So that they can be moved fore and aft, most of these fairleads or blocks rest on tracks. These leads must be set in the right position along the track in order to create the proper airfoil shape all the way along the luff of the sail, from the tack to the head.

If the fairlead is too far aft, it will make the foot, or bottom, of the sail stretch too tight without pulling down along the leech, or trailing edge, of the sail. Without tension on the leech, the head and upper part of the sail will not conform to the airfoil configuration that you have created along the lower luff.

If the fairlead block is too far forward, the sheet will pull down on the leech of the sail without stretching the foot of the sail enough. This will cause the sail to luff along the lower third of its area long before it will luff on the upper third. You must set your fairleads at some position which you feel is approximately right and adjust them once you're out sailing. The more experience you have, the more accurate this first guess will become.

Now, trim the sail in until it is luffing and slowly turn the boat into the wind. Notice where the sail starts luffing first. If the sail luffs along its entire length from the tack to the head, the sheet lead is perfect. If the sail starts to luff at the head first, or near the head, you must

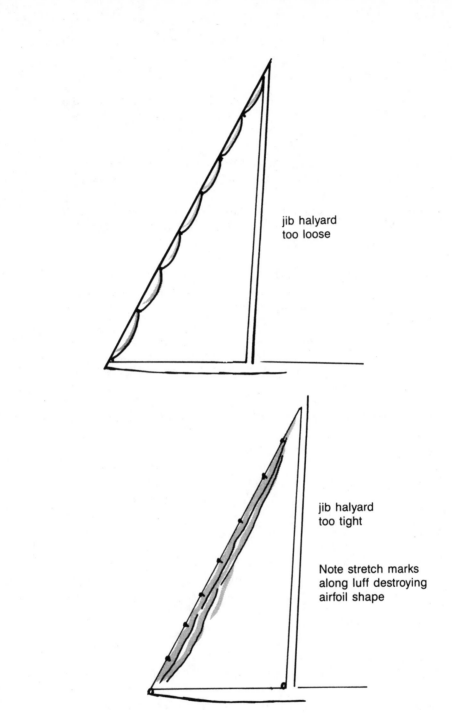

jib halyard
too loose

jib halyard
too tight

Note stretch marks
along luff destroying
airfoil shape

Checking jib halyard tension.

The jib fairlead is too far aft and the bottom third of the sail is too flat; the center third is properly trimmed and the top third is luffing.

move the sheet lead forward to get the same airfoil curve all the way along the length of the sail. If the sail starts to luff along the bottom third of the sail before the top third luffs, then you must move the fairlead further aft to stretch the foot of the sail tighter, giving you the proper airfoil shape along the sail.

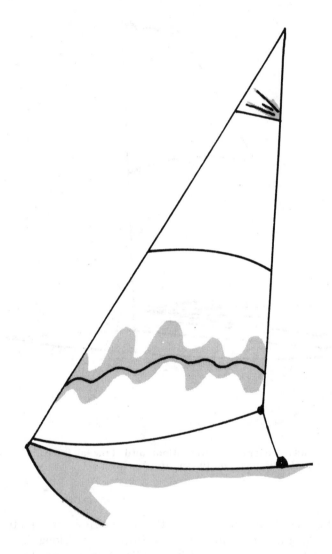

The jib fairlead is too foward and the bottom third of the sail luffs; the center third is properly trimmed and the top third is too flat.

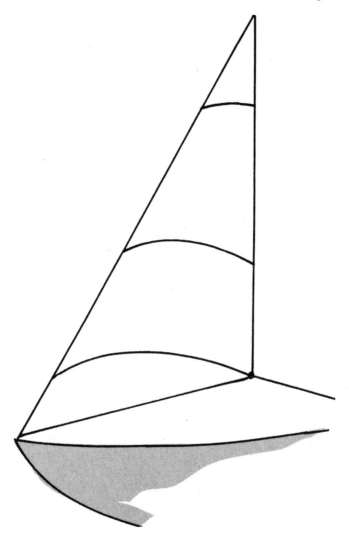

The proper jib sheet lead lets the whole sail assume a proper airfoil shape when trimmed.

It's an interesting fact that pretty sails are usually well-trimmed sails. When you're out sailing, look at your neighbor's boat. Is his jib full of scallops? Is his jib luffing at the top or at the bottom while the rest of the sail is fully drawing? Use these observations of other people's boats to look more carefully at your own. Sometimes you're so close to the trees you can't see the forest. And being so close to your sails makes it difficult to find the proper trim. On many boats, as you go from close-hauled and beating to a beam reach, to running, in order to have the sails trimmed for absolute accuracy, the lead blocks must be moved either slightly forward or slightly aft. Exactly the same principle about the top third of the sail luffing before the bottom third of the sail applies in these new positions for your sail. Unless they are heavily involved in racing, most sailors do not bother changing the lead position from beating, reaching, and running, as the changes are usually quite small.

The Mainsail

In trimming the mainsail, you run into a different series of problems; the mainsail is attached to the mast all along the luff, and attached to the boom all the way along the foot. The mainsail is also aft of the jib and receives disturbed air spilling out of the jib over its surface. This makes it more difficult to trim the mainsail properly. That's why you always trim the jib first. The sail that gets the wind first gets trimmed first. Then the air that spills out of the jib can be used to trim the mainsail correctly.

In raising the mainsail, you must take the same care that the halyard tension is proper that you did with the jib. Get the sail up tight enough so that it is not full of scallops, but not so tight that you destroy the airfoil shape or stretch your sail out of shape. How tight the halyard should be drawn must be determined through experience with your own boat. Watch the sail; try to get it set on the boom and the mast so that you get the fewest wrinkles when the sail is full of wind.

The outhaul helps control the shape of the mainsail by pulling the foot of the sail along the boom. Again, the outhaul must be tight enough to remove the wrinkles from the foot of the sail, but not so tight as to destroy the airfoil shape. A good rule of thumb is: the harder the wind blows, the tighter the halyard and the tighter the outhaul must be.

When the mainsail is up and the halyard and outhaul properly cleated down, you can trim it the same way you trim the jib. Ease the sail out until it luffs; trim it in until it stops luffing.

Battens

Most sails have three or four battens to stiffen the trailing edge, or leech, of the sail and keep it from fluttering. These battens must

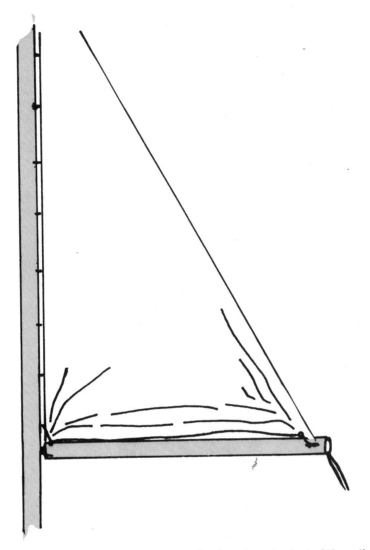

With the outhaul too tight, stretch lines develop along the foot of the sail.

be of the proper length so that they fit snugly in their pockets, but not so long that they stretch the material and cause a wrinkle. The forward end of the battens are normally tapered so that they will bend and conform to the airfoil shape of the sail. When you insert the battens, make sure you put the tapered end in first. Keep the thick, less flexible end aft along the outer edge of the sail to keep the leech stiff.

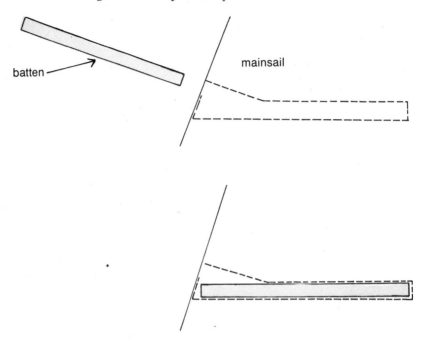

Proper batten installation.

Travelers

Many boats have travelers – devices that allow you to trim the mainsail properly and more easily. A traveler is nothing more than a sliding block on a track that is attached to the boat so that the block can move from port to starboard. The block is part of the mainsheet and makes the mainsheet pull down on the boom more than it pulls in on the boom. It's important to pull down on the boom. When you are sailing on a beam reach, the wind filling the sail tends to make the boom rise up; this rising of the boom destroys the airfoil shape of the sail. If you have a traveler, you can move the block out to make the mainsheet pull down on the boom more directly while sailing on a reach; when you go back onto a beat close to the wind, you can move the traveler block amidships, or even slightly to windward. The mainsheet will pull down on the boom, giving you far better sail shape.

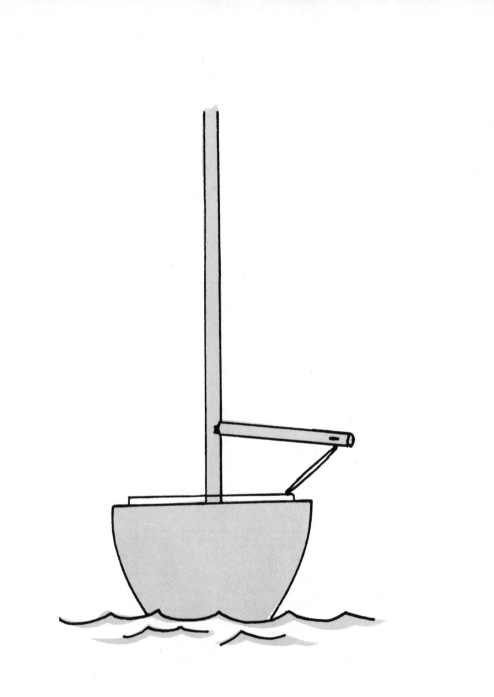

Mainsheet position on the traveler when sailing on a reach.

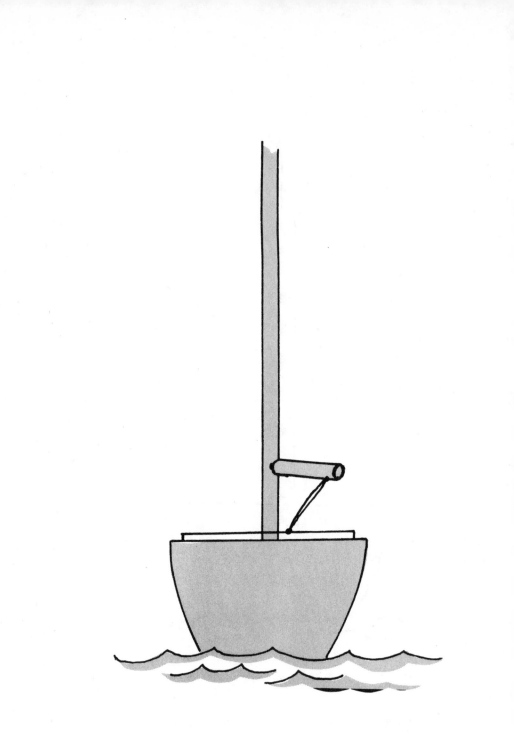

Mainsheet position on the traveler when beating.

Boom Vangs

The purpose of a boom vang is to keep the boom from lifting. The standard installation of a boom vang is from the base of the mast upward to the bottom of the boom at an angle of about 45 degrees. If the vang is set while beating, you can swing the boom all the way out onto a broad reach, or even running dead downwind, and the vang will keep the boom from lifting since it is installed on a true arc of the boom. The vang will help keep this airfoil shape all the way up the forward edge of the sail.

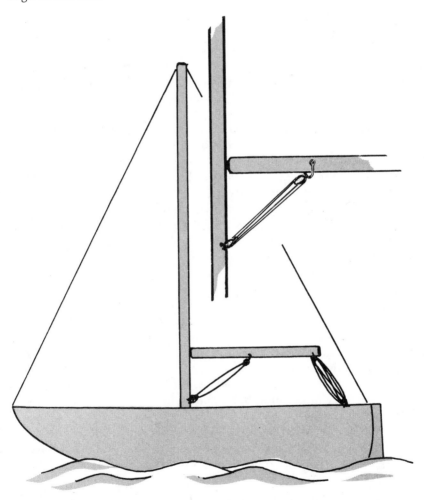

A boom vang installed to the base of the mast.

Many sailors use the vang to bend the boom while beating to windward which helps flatten out the sail. When reaching and running, they ease off the vang in order to get a draftier, or baggier, sail. Masts are also bent in the same manner to get a flatter sail for going to windward and a draftier sail for a reach or a run. These techniques should be used only on racing boats while they're being raced. They have little value to the cruising yachtsman or daysailor; but you should know about them, and now you do.

ANCHORING

The anchor is probably the most valuable tool on your boat, but many sailors don't know how to use it to their best advantage. Always have your anchor accessible for emergency use. If you ever have difficulty at sea, you can drop your sails and sit at anchor until you've fixed the problem; then raise your sails and sail away.

There are many types of anchors available today. The most common are the Danforth and the plow-type anchors. They both have advantages and disadvantages. They hold better than many others; and after you are through using them to hold, they come up better from various bottom conditions. My advice to the new sailor would be to see what anchors friends sailing in your area are using. You might need a grapnel, a folding anchor, a yachtsman's anchor, or a Northill anchor. Your choices are so numerous that it is impossible to suggest one.

One thing to look for, though, is the ease of stowing. If your anchor cannot be stowed easily and properly, you will stick it down in the bilge somewhere, forget about it, and never use it. The easiest and most readily accessible way is to stow the anchor on its own small bowsprit or anchor sprit on the bow of the boat. Many fiberglass boats are being produced with anchor wells on the foredeck of the boat in which you can store your anchor and anchor rode, or line, and get it completely out of the way. Stowing an anchor in chocks on the foredeck is another convenient method. But I have found that they eat your toe every time you walk by, and at times they interfere with your jib and jib sheets.

Wherever you sail, and whatever type of boat you have, check with your local marine dealer. They are usually very helpful in advising you on the proper size and type of anchor gear used in the area in which you intend to sail.

The small centerboard daysailor, of course, will use an anchor far smaller than that of the 25- to 35-foot full-keeled or swing-keeled cruis-

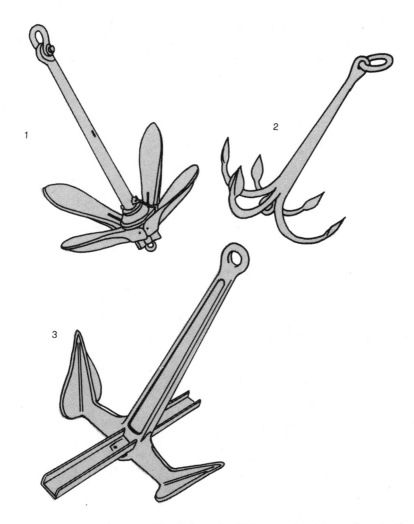

Some common anchors. (1) The flukes of a folding anchor (shown here in the open position) can be snugged up against its shank, secured with a ring, and stowed in a minimum of space. Reopened and tossed overboard, the folding anchor, like the grapnel, is most effective when it hooks rock or coral. Many boatmen take these convenient folding anchors for spares, and some racing sailors conform to class-boat rules by carrying lightweight models. (2) The grapnel, with its multiple sharp tines symmetrically arranged around the crown, can catch on rough rock, coral, or matted weeds. Some fishermen use grapnels as temporary anchors, or "lunch hooks," since on most bottoms they will take a quick – though not necessarily permanent – hold. (3) The lightweight Northill anchor, once standard equipment for tethering seaplanes, has a stock at the crown end that slides out and folds up against the shank for stowing. In use, when one of the sharp flukes sinks into soft mud, the stock will dig in and take hold as well, reinforcing the anchor's grip.

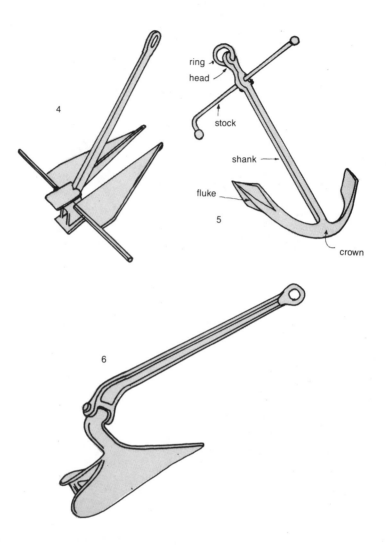

4

ring
head
stock

shank

fluke

5

crown

6

Some common anchors *(continued)*. (4) The kedge, called a yachtsman anchor, is a versatile heavyweight (commonly weighing 25 to 75 pounds) that can hold securely on any kind of bottom – depending upon the width of its flukes. Narrow flukes hold on coral, rocks, and hard sand; a hook with wider flukes, sometimes called a Herreshoff anchor, holds better in softer bottoms. (5) The lightweight (2½ pounds and up) Danforth is excellent for small- and medium-sized boats. Especially effective in sand or mud, the broad-based flukes respond to horizontal pull on the hinged shank by digging down, often burying the whole hook. The stock at the crown end, is in the same plane as the flukes, so the anchor stows flat. (6) The middleweight plow anchor buries itself readily in soft mud and is also effective in penetrating weeds and shell beds. Moreover, a hinge on the shank helps the plow to remain buried when the angle of pull on the rode changes with shifts in wind or current.

ing boat. The full-sized cruising boat should always have a minimum of two anchors, preferably a combination of types, plus a light one to use as a "lunch hook." A lunch hook is a small anchor that you can use when you are stopping for just a short while and aren't leaving the boat unattended. The ease of setting and retrieving the smaller anchor will make the investment pay off rapidly.

Most small boats today have auxiliary power of some sort, either a small outboard or, on larger boats, an inboard engine. Anchoring under power is very similar to anchoring under sail. First, get your anchor and anchor line on the bow of the boat and ready to launch. Make sure the bitter end of the anchor rode is attached to the bow cleat or some other permanent fixture on the boat. The bitter end, of course, is the end of the line that goes sailing overboard with your expensive anchor unless you tie it down. Put the anchor in a position where it can be lowered easily over the side, and flake out the anchor rode so that it will run out smoothly without knotting, kinking, or grabbing your ankle in one of the coils.

Whether you're under sail or under power when you approach your anchorage, you must point the boat directly into the wind and coast to a stop. The man on the bow should watch either the bottom, if the water is clear enough, or a little bubble on the surface so that he can tell if the boat has stopped. If there's no little bubble to watch, he can make one by dipping the anchor in the water.

If you drop the anchor before you have stopped, you're going to run over the line with the keel or centerboard. You might even go so far as to get the anchor line caught in your engine propeller. So, make sure that the boat has stopped, and then lower the anchor. Do not toss the anchor. If you do, the anchor line might catch on one of the flukes or projections on the anchor, and it will never dig into the bottom properly.

Lower the anchor down. If you are under power at this time, the helmsman can reverse the engine and back off until three to four times the water depth in which you are anchoring has been paid out in anchor line from the boat. At this time, snub the anchor line around the bow cleat; the anchor should then set itself. If you are under power, the helmsman then puts the boat in reverse hard to set the anchor while the man on the bow feels the line to make sure that the anchor is not dragging.

If you are under sail and you are just coasting backward, the maneuver can be difficult. The man on the bow has to yank heavily and repeatedly on the anchor line to set it into the bottom. Anchors do not hold onto the bottom by their sheer weight. Sailors call them "hooks" because they literally hook the bottom and hold the boat by

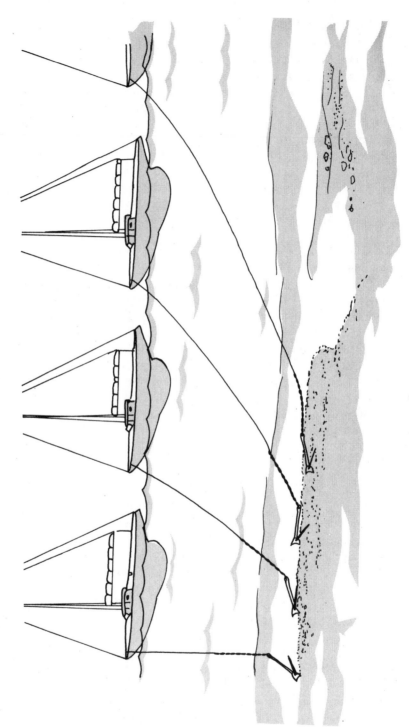

Enough scope is essential to make any anchor hold.

taking a large bite into the mud or sand and rocks or whatever you have on the bottom.

After you have your anchor down, your engine off, and your sails secured, it is often a good idea once again to go up and yank on the anchor line to see if you really have hooked the bottom. Whenever I can, I snorkel down and check my anchor firsthand. If weather and water conditions permit, it's a good habit to get into. It's difficult to do in the arctic in January. But in the Virgin Islands, most prudent skippers do it year-round.

In anchoring either under sail or under power, the man on the bow handling the anchor must tell the helmsman which direction to steer, whether to speed up or slow down, and finally, to secure and cut the engines. It's often amusing to watch what happens when novice sailors come into a crowded anchorage. Because of the engine noise, the man in the cockpit can't hear the orders which the man on the bow yells to him. The frustration this causes can lead to very entertaining conflicts. A simple set of hand signals used by the man in the bow to the helmsman could eliminate this difficulty. Hand signals make anchoring easier, smoother, and far quieter. Check the illustrations for explanations of hand signals.

Raising anchor before sailing away is done pretty much the same under power and under sail. Under power, you motor slowly ahead, again obeying hand signals from the man on the bow. Take up the anchor line until it is vertical. At this point, it's usually easy for the man on the bow to break the anchor out of the bottom and pull it straight up. However, if the anchor is firmly imbedded, you might not be able to pull the anchor right out.

If the anchor does balk, take in as much slack on the anchor line as you possibly can and cleat it on the bow of the boat. Then the man at the helm powers ahead slightly. This should break the anchor out of the mud. The man on the bow can then pull it straight up. Once it's up you can power away.

If the anchor won't come out by using power against it, there are other things you can do. One of these is to get everybody up forward in the boat to push the bow into the water as far as it will go with body weight. Take up all the slack you can with the anchor line and cleat it down on the bow. Then if everyone moves to the stern, the buoyancy of the boat will help the anchor break free from the bottom. Sometimes jumping up and down on the stern in unison will help.

This same technique can be used under sail, except it is best to put up only your mainsail so that it will luff. The man on the bow can pull the boat forward on the anchor line until he is directly over the anchor. He can then break the anchor out and pull it up. After you get the

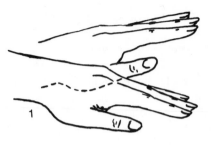

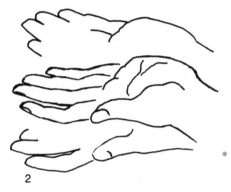

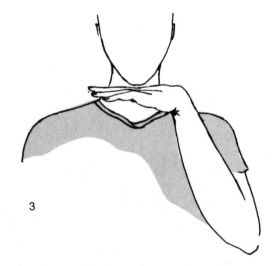

Hand signals used in anchoring. (1) Slow down. Move hand up and down, palm down. (2) Speed up. Move hand up and down, palm up. (3) Stop (put in neutral). Make cutting motion with hand across throat.

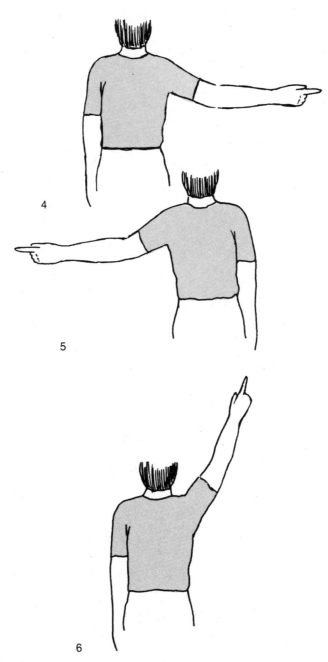

Hand signals used in anchoring *(continued)*. (4) Go more starboard. Point to the starboard with whole arm. (5) Go more port. Point to the port with whole arm. (6) Go ahead. Point ahead with whole arm.

Hand signals used in anchoring *(continued)*. (7) Secure. Repeat stop two or more times. (8) Go astern. Point astern with whole arm.

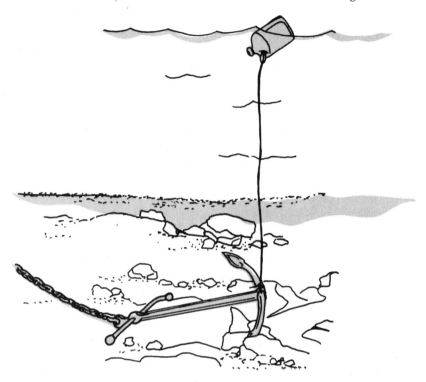

In one method of prerigging an anchor, a so-called tripping line is tied to the anchor's crown and buoyed to the surface. If a fluke becomes jammed, a vertical tug on the line will lift the anchor straight out.

anchor secured on the deck, you can start sailing away under the main and raise the jib.

If you are in extremely rocky territory, or if there is a lot of foul ground – coral, old cable, tree trunks – that your anchor can get hooked on, it is an excellent idea when you are anchoring to put a trip line on your anchor. This is a line from the crown or back end of the anchor to a float on the surface. If the hook is caught on something, perhaps trapped under a rock or tree trunk, you can take the buoy line and lift the anchor backwards exactly as it went in.

REVIEW QUESTIONS

(Answers follow part 7)

1. What is the first thing to do when you hear the cry, "Man overboard"?

2. Is it better to come about or jibe when returning to a man overboard?
3. What happens if the jib halyard is not tight enough?
4. Which part of the sail will be more inclined to luff if the jib lead is set too far forward?
5. Which part of the sail will be more inclined to luff if the jib lead is set too far aft?
6. What happens when the main halyard is too tight?
7. What is the advantage of a traveler?
8. What is the main purpose of the boom vang?
9. What is a lunch hook?
10. What signal is used to tell the helmsman to slow down?

SAILING EXERCISE III

Rig your boat from memory and then refer to the checklist from part 1 to be sure you did it in the right order. You can now leave the dock and sail on all points of sail for a short while to refresh your memory about the exercises from parts 1 and 2.

Put your boat on an easy beam reach and then throw a floating object, such as a boat fender or life jacket, overboard. Proceed to jibe and pick up this man overboard. Practice the man overboard drill five or six times until you have it down perfectly. Repeat the man overboard drill, but now do it starting from a run or when beating to windward.

Remember, at the cry, "man overboard," you must immediately come to a reach. Simulate picking a heavy man from the water; see what method would work best on your boat. It's better to practice now than to panic later.

Adjust your jib leads forward and back while on a beat, a reach, and a run. Adjust the halyard tension on both the main and the jib. Adjust the outhaul on the main and see how all of these adjustments affect sail shape.

Now try to get the sails to look perfect: no wrinkles and a nice airfoil shape. Note how the boom vang will change sail shape on all points of sailing.

You aren't done yet. You still have to anchor. Try anchoring under sail and, if you have an engine, under power. Be careful that there are no lines over the side that can be tangled in the propeller.

After anchoring three or four times, return to the harbor. You've earned a rest.

4

Facing the Elements

BOAT BALANCE

You may have heard about the importance of proper boat balance, but what exactly is it? Simply stated, it is the ability to set the sails and the rudder amidships and have the boat sail a straight course. There are three major factors affecting boat balance: sail trim, centerboard position or distribution of the weight of the crew, and heeling. These three factors must be controlled to keep the boat in balance.

Imagine the sailboat as a weather vane. It pivots in the middle; there is a jib in the front like the pointer on the vane, and there is a mainsail on the back like the large blade of the vane. Both of these two ends can be pushed by the wind. As the wind blows against them, the boat can pivot into or out of the wind unless the force of the wind acting on the sails is properly balanced.

Naval architects and designers have special terms for the points in the sails and on the boat affected by these forces. The pivot point on the hull is the "center of lateral resistance." At this point you could attach a line and pull the boat sideways — laterally — and neither the bow nor the stern would come off the perpendicular. The wind affects the sails most at the "center of effort." It's as if somebody were taking one finger and pushing the sails at this point.

When you're sailing on a beam reach, the center of lateral resistance is approximately below the center of effort in the sails. If you take down the jib, the center of effort moves back into the center of the mainsail. Since the new center of effort is now far behind the center of lateral resistance, the boat is unbalanced. The wind will push against the rear-sail which turns the boat on its pivot point and pushes the bow up into the wind.

If you drop the mainsail and put the jib up, the center of effort will be in the middle of the jib. Since this center of effort is far forward of the center of lateral resistance, or pivot point, the wind will push the bow of the boat out of the wind.

You don't have to drop the mainsail or the jib to achieve these changes. You can get the same effect by letting the sails luff. If you let the jib luff, the mainsail will take over and push the boat up into the wind. If you let the mainsail luff, the jib will take over and push the boat out of the wind. By trimming and easing sails, you can easily steer the boat without using the rudder. Simply ease or trim the sails in and out as needed to bring you up into or out of the wind.

Poorly trimmed sails are the major cause of boat imbalance. The second major cause is displacement of the center of lateral resistance. On a boat with a centerboard you can move the center of lateral resistance aft by raising the centerboard slightly. While you sacrifice only a small portion of the exposed area of the centerboard, the center of lateral resistance, or pivot point, is moved aft quite a bit. The further aft you move the pivot point, the more sail area there will be forward of the pivot point. This of course, will push your bow out of the wind.

On a boat without a centerboard, you can move the center of lateral resistance by moving your crew weight forward or aft. Moving the crew forward pushes the bow into the water, giving you more lateral resistance forward. Now you have more sail area behind the center of lateral resistance to push the bow of the boat up into the wind. Moving your crew weight aft will push the stern deeper into the water, giving you more lateral resistance aft and allowing the bow to be pushed out of the wind.

The third factor affecting boat balance is heeling. When the boat is standing straight up and down in the water, the water flow is equal over the two curved sides of the boat. However, as the boat heels over, one side of the boat becomes immersed deeper into the water causing imbalance. The water passing over the curved section of the immersed hull creates greater rudder-like effect. So, the further the boat heels

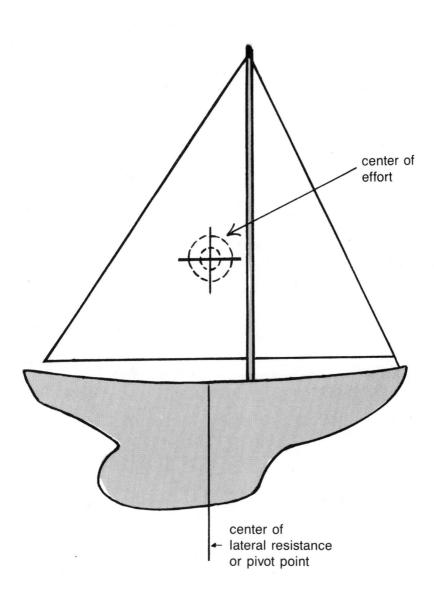

center of
effort

center of
← lateral resistance
or pivot point

The boat is balanced when the center of effort is approximately in line with the pivot point.

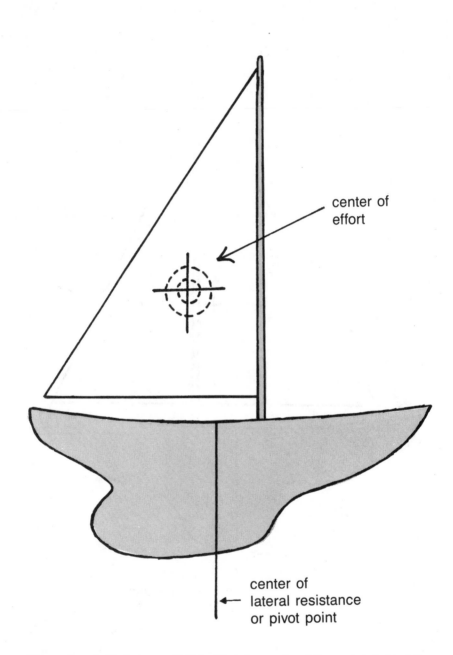

center of
effort

center of
lateral resistance
or pivot point

The center of effort moves aft if the jib is lowered and the push is behind the pivot point.

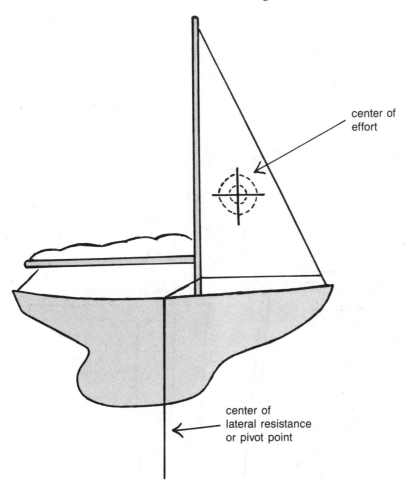

center of
effort

center of
lateral resistance
or pivot point

The center of effort is forward of the pivot point, pushing the bow out of the wind.

over, the greater the tendency for the boat to come up into the wind or into the weather. This isn't really all bad. If you take a sudden puff and are being overpowered, the boat will turn up into the wind, the sails will luff, the boat will straighten up, and you can steer back on course.

The worst case I've ever seen of complete disregard for all of the principles involved in boat balance was dropped in my lap several years ago. An inexperienced sailor bought a new 34-foot keel, centerboard sloop and had it commissioned at the yard I was managing. After his initial sail, he complained that the boat had bad weather helm and

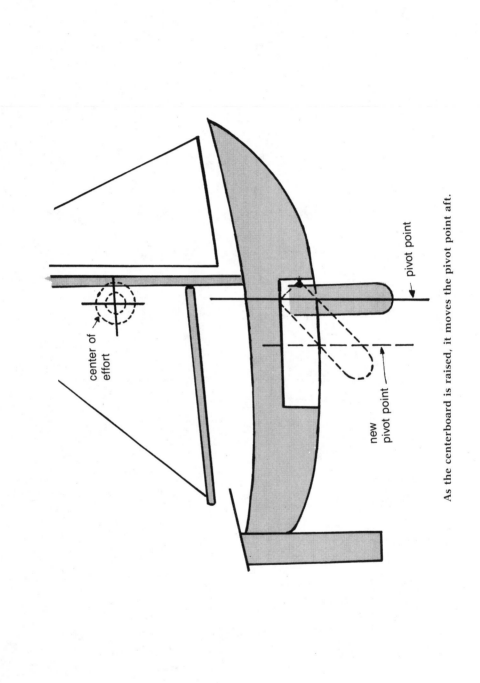

center of
effort

pivot point

new
pivot point

As the centerboard is raised, it moves the pivot point aft.

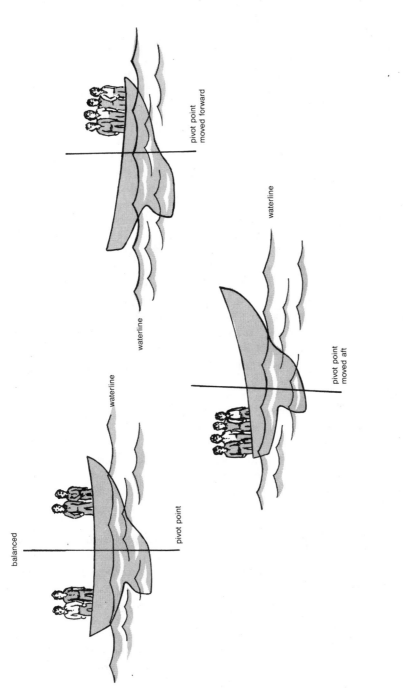

Shifting crew weight produces more area underwater, forward or aft, changing the center of lateral resistance forward or aft.

that I should rake the mast forward to correct it. After we had raked the mast forward following three successive Sunday sails, the boat still had terrible weather helm according to the owner. When I sold him the boat, I thought it had a slight lee helm; it tended to turn out of the wind. I was finally able to corner the owner with some additional questions on just what was happening while he was sailing. The conversation went something like this:

Q. What course were you on?
A. I was beating to windward.
Q. Why didn't you raise the board slightly to move the pivot point aft? That would give you more sail area forward to push the bow out of the wind and cure your weather helm.
A. I was beating to windward and didn't want to side slip. (He forgot that I said raise the centerboard slightly so that you don't lose that much area.)
Q. Where were your crew?
A. They were all in the cockpit. (They should have been on the windward rail to reduce heeling.)
Q. What sails did you have up?
A. My main and working jib.
Q. Why didn't you put up the genoa to get more sail area forward?
A. It was blowing too hard.
Q. Why didn't you reef the main to reduce the sail area aft?
A. It wasn't blowing that hard.
Q. Well why didn't you put up the genoa and reef the main?
A. It was too much work.

Yes, the boat did have bad weather helm. It was sailed with the wrong centerboard setting, crew position, and sail combination, and it was so out of balance that it was no fun to sail. The story does have a happy ending. The owner sold the boat at a substantial loss since he told everyone about the bad weather helm; the new owner put the mast back where it belonged, sailed the boat properly, and went on to win many races. There are far more bad sailors than there are bad boats.

The next time you go out, try sailing as straight a course as you can. Shift your crew weight from one side of the boat to the other; see how you can bring the boat up into the wind by increasing the heeling and bring it back out of the wind by decreasing the heeling. Practice lashing the rudder amidships and trimming and luffing your sails to get where you want to go. It's a good trick, and it might get you back home sometime when you've had steering problems.

When you're trying to come about in light winds with very little steerage way, you can use the sails and boat balance to help you steer. Release your jib as soon as you start to come about, and trim your mainsail in flat. The mainsail will then push you up into and through the wind, at which time you can backwind the jib – that is, trim the jib on the wrong side so that it is backed into the wind. The backed

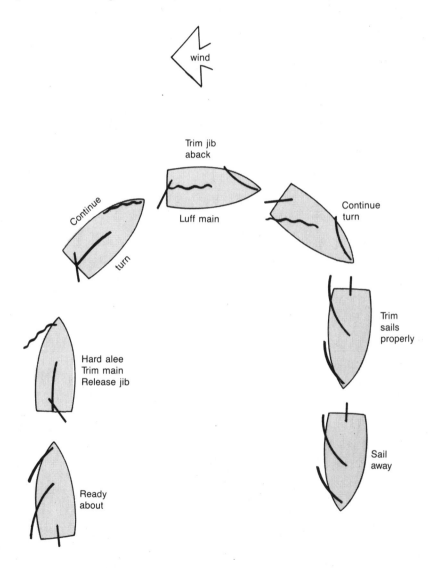

Coming about in light winds using the sails to help you turn.

jib will finish pushing the bow of the boat around. At that time you can release the jib, trim it in properly, and go on your way. It is very important to know the effects of the wind upon your sails when you're trying to steer in tight quarters.

Another balance trick that you can use when you're sailing short-handed is to sail on a reach and back the jib—that is, trim it to windward. People will look at you and say, What in the world is that boat doing with its jib trimmed improperly? However, this will put your main and your jib in opposition to each other and make the boat self-steering. The boat will remain self-steering either until the wind changes direction, at which time the boat will change direction, or until the wind changes velocity, which will cause the boat to heel over more and bring you up in the wind. You won't be going as fast sailing with the jib backed, but it will give you an opportunity to leave the tiller and go below, or forward, or wherever you wish for a few minutes.

In order for a boat to sail properly and comfortably, all three of the major factors in boat balance must be in tune with one another. The sailor who truly knows and understands boat balance can use it to get himself out of all kinds of trouble.

RUNNING AGROUND

Running downwind is the worst situation you can be in when you run aground. When you are running downwind, the wind is behind you and pushing you harder and harder onto the shoal area. You must reverse your course and move your boat out in the direction you came from. It is impossible to sail off a shoal in this situation. The main must be dropped immediately to spill the wind out of it so that it doesn't drag you further and further onto the shoal. And an anchor must be taken from the boat directly aft and out to windward. You can row the anchor out in the dinghy or swim it out, floating the anchor on a life jacket. Where the shoal is not steep-sided, you can just wade out until you are neck deep in water and drop the anchor there.

After the anchor is set, turn the boat around—one person pulling on the anchor line and the other person in the water pushing on the hull. After the boat is turned directly into the wind and being held by the anchor line, let the action of the winds break the keel free from the bottom. If the waves won't work for you, have the person in the water push on the boat, or have the people on the boat lean over to heel the boat over to one side. Once the boat is free from the bottom, pull forward on the anchor line as fast as possible to get headway. You can sail away on a close reach under jib alone until you get further from the shoal and have time to put up the mainsail.

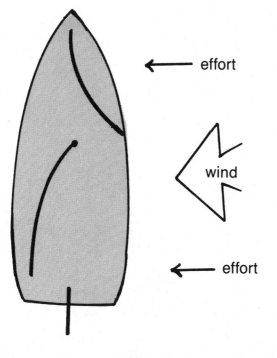

If the mainsail is squarer to the wind, it will pivot the bow into the wind making the jib squarer to the wind and more effective in turning the bow back out of the wind. As the jib becomes squarer to the wind, the converse happens and we are in balance until the wind shifts or the angle of heel changes.

For too long too many people have taught that when you run aground you have to heel the boat over and sail it off the shoal. If you are aground with the shallow water to leeward, the more you heel the boat over, the further onto the shoal the wind will push you. The only way to get off the shoal when it is to leeward is to pull yourself off with your own anchor, get a tow from somebody else's boat, or use your own engine to power out.

When a boat runs aground while sailing on an approximate beam reach, the simplest way to get off is to turn the boat around and sail off in the direction you came from. First, luff the jib and trim the mainsail in as tight as you can amidships. Normally, the boat will weather vane and pivot on its keel. When it comes head to wind, you can use a paddle or a pole to push the boat through the wind. Back the jib in order to get the jib to fill, and continue to turn the boat around 180 degrees. If you now trim both the main and the jib in flat and get all your crew weight to leeward, you should heel over far enough to break

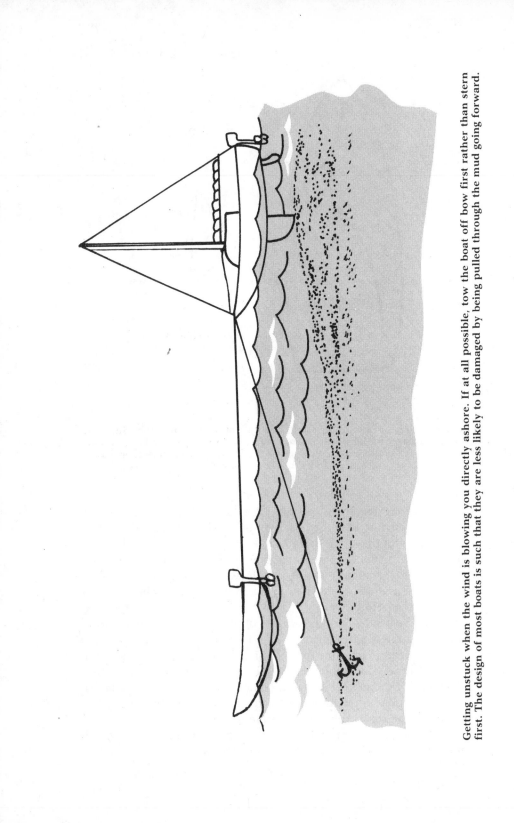

Getting unstuck when the wind is blowing you directly ashore. If at all possible, tow the boat off bow first rather than stern first. The design of most boats is such that they are less likely to be damaged by being pulled through the mud going forward.

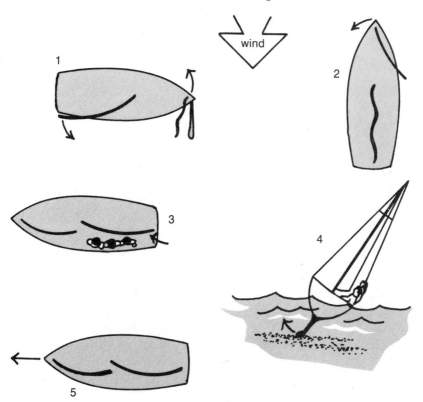

Getting unstuck when you run aground with the wind abeam. (1) Turn the boat. Push with an oar. (2) Backwind jib. (3) Sails tight. All crew to leeward. (4) Heel the boat. (5) Sail off.

out of the mud, get the boat moving, and sail away in the direction you came from.

As long as the bottom is not full of coral rocks, running aground while beating is usually not a big problem for a modern sailboat. If you are sailing as close into the wind as you can when you run aground, the wind itself will tend to push you back off the shoal. You can assist the wind by backing the jib. This will turn the boat perpendicular to the wind and heel it over far enough to let you sail off on the other side.

An old sailor once told me, "The best way to get off the bottom when you are run aground is not to run aground in the first place." A little bit of attention and vigilance can save you hours of anxiety and sometimes can even save damage to your boat.

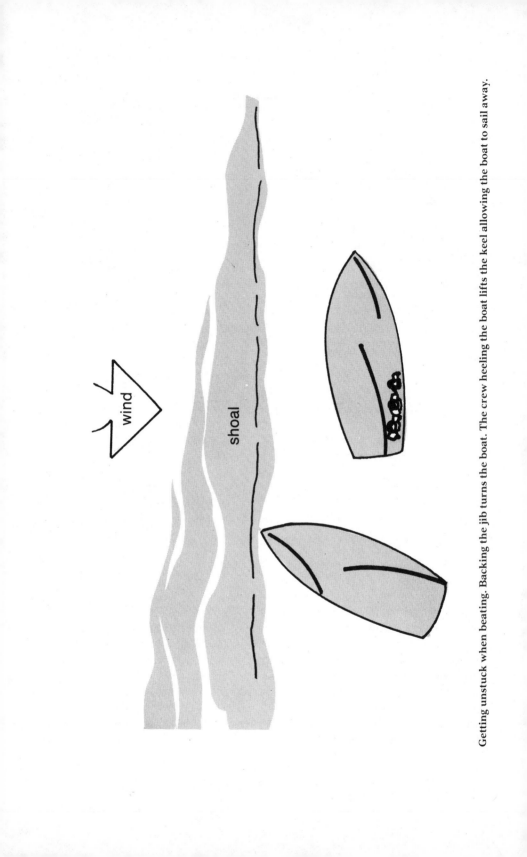

Getting unstuck when beating. Backing the jib turns the boat. The crew heeling the boat lifts the keel allowing the boat to sail away.

HEAVY WEATHER

You don't usually plan to go out sailing in heavy weather. But occasionally the weather changes while you're out there, and suddenly you'd better know something about heavy-weather sailing.

Rain alone doesn't do much except get you wet. The best way to protect yourself against rain problems is to button up the boat, make sure your hatches are closed, put on your foul weather gear, turn your pipe upside down and continue to sail.

Rain reduces visibility, however. So before the rain really sets in, take an accurate compass reading on a visual landmark you can head for. If you stay on that heading throughout the rainstorm, you can stay out of trouble and on course. Estimate your time of arrival at the known distance. If the object does not come into view before you've used up all that time, reverse course and go back the same way. Sometimes you can anchor until visibility improves.

Rain combined with lightning and thunder is another situation entirely. We all know that thunder doesn't hurt you, but it sure does scare you. It scares me. Lightning should not cause any trouble to a modern, well-built sailboat where the mast and shrouds are grounded through the keel or centerboard or through a large ground plate in the hull of the boat. When they're grounded properly, the mast and shrouds form a cone of protection over the boat. Lightning rarely strikes a sailboat. Look at the large number of boats that are tied up day and night in modern marinas. It seems they're never struck by lightning. I'm not pooh-poohing the danger of lightning. It's not a good policy to go out in a thunder storm. But when you are caught out there in a storm, you are safer on a sailboat than you would be standing under a tree on a golf course – as long as you have your boat grounded and you stay away from the shrouds, mast, and other metal fittings on the boat.

Reefing

The real problem in heavy-weather sailing is wind. Wind causes waves. The combination of high winds and large waves creates problems for the small boat sailor. There are many ways you can reduce the effects of heavy wind and waves on the boat. The first is to reduce your sail area by reefing.

Reefing is a method of reducing the area of sail so that the wind doesn't overpower you. The quickest and easiest way to reef is to change headsails. If you have a large jib up, drop the jib and change to a working jib or storm jib. If you have a roller reefing jib, roll it up. You can

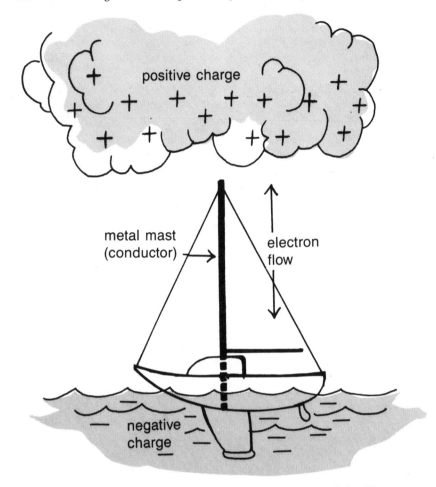

A cone of protection is provided on a properly grounded sailboat.

always take it out a little at a time as you see what the true velocity of the wind is when the storm hits. Try to be a weather prophet. The more you know about your local weather, the easier it will be to be prepared for it. Keep an eye on the horizon for any approaching thunder storms or squalls. Make your changes before the storm hits. It is far easier to change sails before the storm breaks than after the storm is upon you.

When they talk about reefing, most sailors are talking about reefing the mainsail. The easiest way to reef is to do it at the dock before you go out. However, if you're already out sailing and the wind comes up, bring the boat up onto a close reach; while you are keeping steerage way through the use of the jib, let your main luff slightly. If you let it luff too much, the main will thrash violently. The boom will jump so much that you won't be able to hang onto it to tie in a reef.

There are three common methods for reefing mainsails that you should know about. The first of these is the old-fashioned, hand-tied reef. Its big advantage is that it is simple. Since there are no moving parts, very little can go wrong and there is nothing to break. All you need are kringles in your sail – large grommets or holes in a line across the sail from luff to leech, parallel to the boom. With the main luffing slightly, lower the main halyard until the reef kringle at the luff of the sail meets the boom. Take a piece of line and tie the kringle down tightly to the boom. There will be a reef kringle along the leech, or trailing edge, of the sail as well. Take another piece of line through the leech kringle and stretch the sail out as tight as it will go; then tie it down tightly to the boom. Your hand-tied reef is now complete. You may sheet the mainsail in and start sailing.

Once you're back in control, you'll have time to gather up all the loose sail hanging down along the boom. There are intermediate reef points – small holes in the sail on a line between the leech reef kringle and the luff reef kringle. Normally, these intermediate points have small reefing lines permanently attached to them. Take these lines and pass them – not around the boom, but between the sail and the boom – and tie them around the furled sail. This will hold the sail out of the way and keep it neatly furled while you are reefed.

One of the biggest mistakes that beginning sailors make in reefing is to tie these intermediate reefing points too tight. These points are there only to keep the sail from falling down. They are not designed to take any strain from the sails. All of the strain is taken at the luff and the leech of the sail with the two major kringles. Take a good look at the way the sail is built; see the size and strength of the reinforcing patches that are sewn in around these two major kringles. The intermediate points have just small square patches sewn into them, and they have no strength at all. If you tie them too tight, I guarantee that you're going to tear your sails. While sailing with the reef in, if you see any sign of strain on the mainsail at these intermediate points, luff immediately and loosen that line. A good rule of thumb is: if you cannot take your clenched fist and pass it through the loop formed by the line around the sail, the intermediate reefing points are tied too tight.

Jiffy reefing is a modern adaptation of the old hand-tied reef. The major difference is that a line is permanently rigged from the boom through the luff kringle and back down to a cleat. A second line is rigged from the boom up to the leech kringle, back to the boom, and forward along the boom to a cleat. This eliminates the need to hand-tie

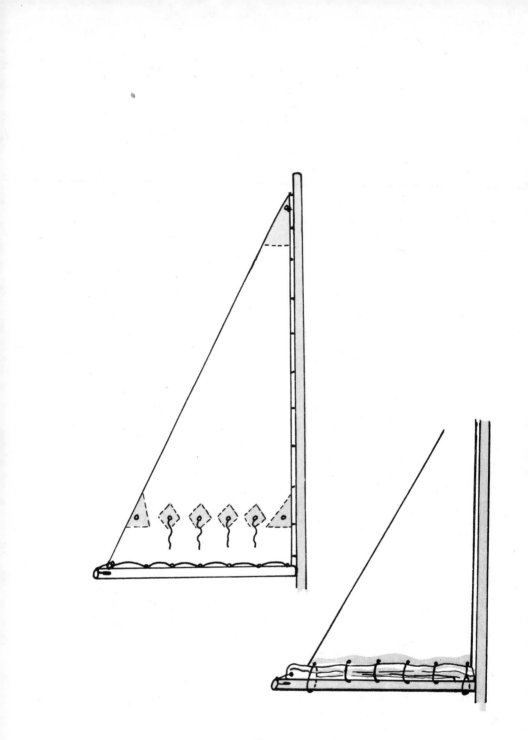

A hand-tied reef.

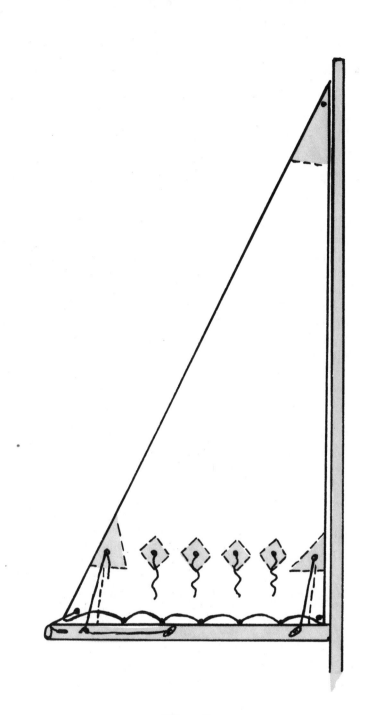

Jiffy reefing.

the luff kringle to the boom and the leech kringle out and down to the boom. As you lower the halyard, the line at the luff of the sail can be pulled tight. As soon as the kringle is down at the boom, the jiffy reefing line can be secured, and tension can be put back on the halyard. At the same time or immediately after, tighten the leech. The leech kringle can be pulled down and out with the jiffy reefing line and secured to the cleat. Some people will tighten the leech kringle first; others will tighten the luff kringle first. Some will do them both at the same time. It all depends on how your boat is rigged and which way is most convenient for your particular boat. After the forward and aft jiffy reefing lines are secured, tie in the intermediate reef points.

The third method of reefing is roller reefing. Roller reefing incorporates special equipment that allows you to furl the mainsail onto the boom like an upside-down window shade. Roller reefing has gone into disfavor recently because of the difficulty in getting the sail to go around the boom properly. Remember that a sail is not flat. Since it has an airfoil shape or draft sewn into it, you wind up with a baggy mess instead of a neatly reefed sail as you try to roll it around the boom. Roller reefing has also fallen into disdain because of all the gears, handles, and winches needed to crank the boom around. These mechanical items tend to catch the sail in the gears and shred it up. Sometimes saltwater corrosion stops it from working altogether. If your mainsheet happens to come into the mid boom area instead of at the end of the boom, as it does on many boats, it is almost impossible to devise a roller reefing system that will work without rolling at the mainsheet along with the sail.

Some of the smallest sailboats use a type of roller reefing that is not geared. Since the boom is spring-loaded to the gooseneck, when you pull the boom aft you can rotate it, and when you push it forward you engage a square peg on the end of the gooseneck to a square hole in the boom; that keeps the reefed sail from unrolling. This is a rather inexpensive approach to an expensive problem. And although it works rather well, sometimes the sail will flog out of its furl if you let it luff violently. If you have this type of reefing system on your boat, I recommend that you take the sail to a sailmaker and have him put in a set of reef points that you can use. Nothing mechanical, nothing to break —a few pieces of line and you can put in a reef.

Avoiding a Capsize

If you have enough maneuvering room when a storm hits, you can sail with the wind slightly forward of the beam so that you can climb

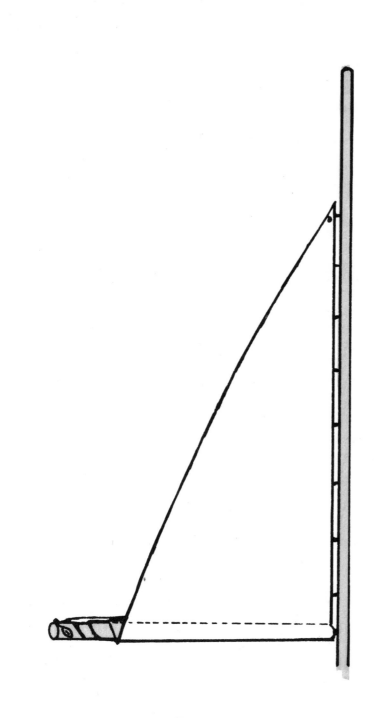

Roller reefing.

a wave on approximately a 45-degree angle and slide down the other side. You cannot go directly into the wind as you might be inclined to do in a powerboat because you cannot sail directly into the wind. You do not want to run with the wind directly on the beam because of the rolling motion as you top these waves. And waves breaking flat on the side of the boat might swamp it. Running downwind in a small boat ahead of large breaking waves is extremely dangerous; the waves can break behind you and completely fill your cockpit. Plus, steering is so difficult as you come to the crest of one wave and down the next one that you might jibe and create a whole new set of problems.

If the water depth allows, the best thing to do before the storm hits is to turn the boat up into the wind and drop your anchor. Then take your sails down, secure them properly, and wait out the storm. Sudden storms are usually quite short-lived. It may be macho to go out and fight the storm, but it is easier and smarter to seek shelter before the storm hits or to anchor and ride it out. If you can do neither, follow the suggestions on reefing and put on your life jacket. If you are sailing in a small boat that is capable of capsize, and if there is any doubt as to the strength of the wind, have the crew don life jackets automatically. It only makes good sense.

Almost all centerboard boat sailors experience a capsize at one time or another. They might capsize because somebody didn't shift his weight from one side of the boat to the other for needed stability when coming about. Or perhaps a sheet stuck to a cleat when it had to be released for a sudden gust of wind. Whatever the reason, some sailors end up capsized. Before this happens to you, have the foresight to secure all loose objects in the boat. That includes the hand bilge pump, the bucket, the icebox, the life jackets – everything in the boat. If you haven't secured these, the first five minutes of your capsize will be spent swimming around trying to collect all the loose gear that starts floating away. Believe me, the best thing to do is secure all the gear before you go out.

Different boats respond in different ways to the efforts of the captain and crew to right them after a capsize. Once a boat goes over, the one common goal is to keep the boat from turning completely upside down. On many of the older centerboard boats with wooden masts, the flotation in the spars is enough to keep the boat floating on its side. But many modern sailboats have aluminum masts which will fill with water and hold the boat upside down. In order to prevent this, the first thing to do in a capsize is to swim to the head of the mast and attach a spare life jacket or cushion to it.

Some boats can be righted immediately – with all the sails still set on the mast and the boom – just by using body weight to counteract

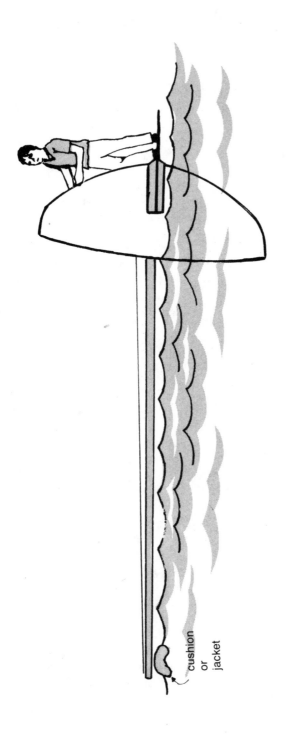

cushion
or
jacket

Righting after a capsize.

the weight of the sails in the water. On other boats, the sail must be lowered and secured to reduce the weight on the upper portion of the boat.

If you have an anchor aboard, it probably will have spilled out already; you can secure the anchor properly with the right length of anchor rode to keep you from drifting from the point of the capsize. That will give you time to straighten out the gear and get things ready to right the boat. It will also hold the bow of the boat approximately into the wind. After the sails have been lowered and secured, and the anchor set, the next step is to get your crew weight pulling down on the centerboard; this will lever the mast up skyward and right the boat.

Some boats are self-bailing once they're upright, and the water will just drain out of them. The crew can get back on the boat, raise the sails, pull up the anchor, and sail away. On boats that are not self-bailing, once they're upright you must bail the rest of the water out of the boat before you can get in. You can bail the boat by splashing some of the water out with a paddle or with your arm, or use a bucket until the water is low enough to let you sneak in over the transom without capsizing the boat. Once aboard, you can bail the rest of the water out.

With today's large array of centerboards that are self-bailing, I don't think it's wise for the beginning sailor to own a boat that is not. Some purists and small boat racers would disagree with me. Self-bailing features often make the boat less competitive because of the added weight of the cockpit and flotation gear necessary. On the other hand, many small boats that are beautiful little racing boats, such as the Laser, are completely self-bailing and can be righted in an instant by one man, remounted, and sailed away with hardly a loss of time.

If by some ill luck your boat does turn upside down on you, and if the mast gets stuck in the mud on the bottom, be extremely careful. If you try to raise the boat up by putting body weight in the centerboard, or by pulling on it with a powerboat, you can easily bend, or even break, the mast. Move the boat so that the top of the mast is pointed directly into the wind; the wind pushing on the half-floating hull should then pull the mast out of the mud. Then, by exerting pressure on the centerboard, you can right the boat.

REVIEW QUESTIONS

(Answers follow part 7)

1. What are the three major factors affecting boat balance?
2. What is the center of lateral resistance?
3. What is the center of effort?

4. Will the boat turn into or out of the wind if the mainsail is allowed to luff?

5. If you raise the centerboard slightly, will the boat turn into or out of the wind?

6. If you move your crew to windward so that the boat sails flatter, will the boat turn into or out of the wind?

7. If you shift your crew weight forward, will the boat turn into or out of the wind?

8. Which is the most difficult point of sailing to re-float from after running aground?

9. In rain or reduced visibility what action should you take when sailing?

10. What should you do *before* the storm hits?

11. In hand-tied or jiffy reefing, how tight should the clew and leech kringle lines be?

12. In hand-tied or jiffy reefing, how tight should the intermediate ties be?

13. In a capsize on a centerboard boat, what is the first thing you should do?

14. What is the best way to get the mast out of the mud if the boat turns upside down?

SAILING EXERCISES IV

By this stage of your sail training, rigging the boat should be a snap. You should now go out and practice boat balance. Put the boat on a beam reach and set the sails properly. Trim in the jib as flat as it can go. Note how you have to make a rudder correction to keep the boat sailing the same course. Now, trim the jib properly, overtrim the mainsail, and watch the boat turn up into the wind.

Shift your crew weight to make the boat heel more or less, and note how it makes the boat change course. Try sailing with the jib backed and the tiller lashed in place. Note how you can make slight course corrections by adjusting the trim of the mainsail or the jib, or changing the amount of heel.

Try to make the boat come about without using the rudder. First, trim in the main flat, and then, when the boat comes head to wind, back the jib to complete the turn. If you can do this without using the rudder, think how valuable this trick will be when you can use the rudder in light winds or where there is a crowded situation.

If you have a sandy area, try running the boat aground and getting the boat free of the bottom again. When doing this, be very careful that you do not damage either the centerboard, keel, or rudder. Practice only in very calm seas, light winds, and with a smooth bottom.

Use your reefing system to reef your mainsail, both at the dock and underway. Take the reef out just by reversing the procedure while underway.

If you own a centerboard daysailor, I want you to capsize your boat and right it. Do this in water shallow enough to stand in and, of course, in light winds and calm seas.

See what problems arise in righting and bailing your boat. Solve these problems before you capsize accidentally under far more severe weather conditions.

If you can't rescue yourself from this capsize, get professional help to teach you how. If you still can't rescue yourself, sell the boat. It isn't safe for you to sail.

5

Keeping an Orderly Ship

KNOTS AND SPLICES

Anyone who sails should know a minimum of four knots. These four are the figure eight, the bowline, the clove hitch and the reef, or square, knot. With these four knots, you can solve almost any problem in tying up or rigging a boat.

Let's start with the figure eight knot. A stopper knot, the figure eight is used at the end of sheets and halyards to keep the line from running out through a block and coming adrift. The figure eight knot is used rather than the standard overhand knot because it will untie easily even when it is pulled taut. If you have hollow base cleats on your mast, it is very convenient to take the end of the halyard, run it through the hollow base of the cleat, and tie a figure eight knot in it for a stopper, guaranteeing that the end of the halyard will not come adrift and suddenly end up at the top of the mast.

The square, or reef, knot is used to tie together two ropes of similar diameter. The only difficulty is that if there is a heavy strain put on the line, the knot is difficult to untie.

The bowline is the sailor's most useful knot. It forms a permanent loop at the end of a line. You can use a bowline with a large loop to

The figure eight knot. (1) Make an underhand loop, bringing the bitter end around and over the standing part. (2) Pass the bitter end under and then up through the loop. (3) Draw the knot up tight.

drop over a piling or bollard when tying up your vessel. It is the preferred knot for pulling people from the water because you can loop it under their arms, and it will not slip down and form a noose. The bowline is probably the most common way of tying your jib sheets onto the clew of the jib. Remember that a reef knot under strain will pull tight and make it difficult to untie. If you know you're going to have a heavy strain on two lines you have to join together, why not tie a bowline on each end and join the lines with the two bowlines. No matter how heavy the strain, the knots will untie easily.

Dock lines should never have eyes spliced into the end of them. If you leave the line plain with just a whipping on either end to keep it from unraveling, you can do anything you want with the line. If there is an eye splice at one end, you can't run it through a pulley, for instance. You also can't get it off the piling if the lines of another boat are tied over yours. If you use a bowline to form a loop over the piling, all you have to do is untie the knot, pull the end of the line, and it comes free. Once you learn how, the bowline is easy to tie – and easy to untie when you no longer need it.

The next knot is the clove hitch. The clove hitch is a quick way of tying a boat fast to a bollard or piling, but tightening and slacking the clove hitch may allow the knot to slip and the boat to come untied. If you tie a clove hitch and are going to leave your vessel for any length of time, I strongly suggest that you bring the bitter end of the line –

The square knot. Work with only one end of the line. (1) Pass the end over and around the other. (2) Bring the ends back together, passing the same end over and around the other. (3) Draw up tight by pulling on both ends.

that is, the end of the line that is not attached to the boat – around to the standing part of the line that runs between the boat and the piling, and tie an additional half hitch. This prevents the line from coming undone in any type of weather.

Modern synthetic lines are easy to work with and to splice. I won't cover splicing lines here because there are so many different types of braided and twisted lines available today. Instructions from the rope manufacturer and special tools are required to splice these modern lines.

Whipping the lines is basically the same on any type of rope. The easiest way to whip a line is to use some sail twine or marline and tightly coil the twine around the line. (For finishing it off, see the illustration

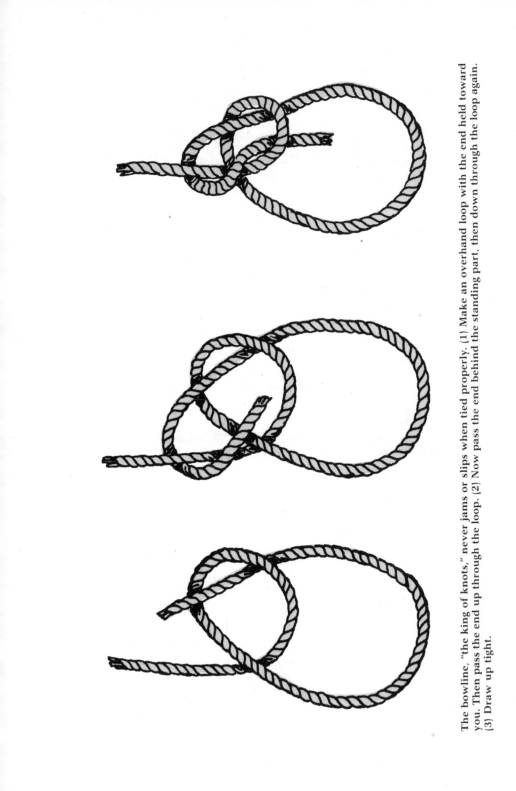

The bowline, "the king of knots," never jams or slips when tied properly. (1) Make an overhand loop with the end held toward you. Then pass the end up through the loop. (2) Now pass the end behind the standing part, then down through the loop again. (3) Draw up tight.

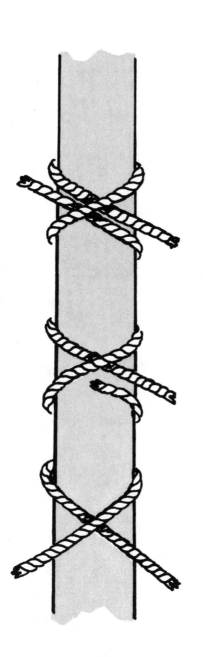

The clove hitch. (1) Make a turn with the rope around the piling and over itself. (2) Take a second turn around the piling. (3) Pull the end up, under the second turn, so that it is parallel to the standing part, the part of the line that leads to the boat, and tighten by pulling on both ends.

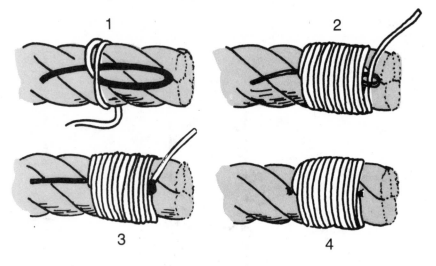

Plain whipping. Lay a loop along the length of the rope. Bind the loop with a series of turns around the rope, pulled against the lay of the rope until you reach a length that is approximately the same length as the diameter of the rope that you are whipping. Place the working end of the whipping line through the loop and, pulling on the remaining part of the loop, neatly slip the entire line snugly under your whipping and cut off both ends.

of plain whipping.) A far better whipping can be done with a sailor's palm and needle. It is not only a stronger and longer lasting whipping but also looks far more seamanlike. A little practice will allow you to whip a line quickly and easily. One advantage to synthetic line in whipping is that the line can be cut with a hot knife or soldering iron. You don't actually cut the line; you melt it in two and at the same time seal all the little fibers of the line together, making it more difficult for the line to unravel.

KEEPING SHIPSHAPE

Nowhere is the adage, "A place for everything and everything in its place," more important than it is on a boat. You should be able to reach any object on your boat in the dark — know exactly where it's stowed and be confident that it is there. As a result, you will be able to find it right away in an emergency or be able to tell anyone else exactly where it can be found. This is nothing more than keeping shipshape. Put the item back when you are through using it — exactly where you found it — and stow the most commonly used things in the most accessible places.

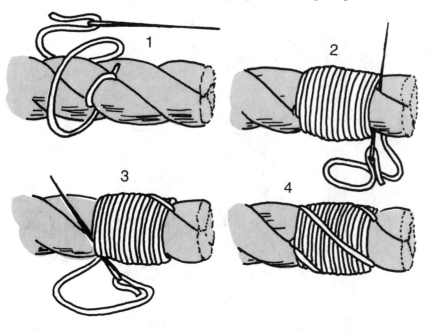

Needle whipping. Needle whipping requires a sailor's palm and sail needle but makes the strongest, neatest whipping of all. First, secure the end of the whipping line by taking a few stitches through the rope that you are whipping. Wrap the sail twine firmly around the line several times until you have used up approximately the same length of rope as the diameter of the rope that you are whipping. Pass the needle under the strand of the rope, down through the groove in the rope, and back under the next strand. Repeat the process until you have worked your way completely around the rope. Secure the end of your twine by stitching it several times through the length of the rope and cut off any excess.

Lines should be coiled, and there are several ways of doing this. The accompanying drawings illustrate two of these – one that is convenient to use on a line that you are coiling to store in a bin, the other to be used on a line that you are coiling to hang on a hook. Anchor lines should, at all times, be flaked out in such a manner that, when the anchor is dropped overboard, the line will run freely out of its compartment.

All cotter pins in your turn buckles, blocks, and shackles should be taped at all times. If you leave the bare cotter pins exposed, they're either going to tear your fingers, your ankles, or your sails at some time.

The little cotter rings that are frequently used, especially in situations where you have to step and unstep your mast frequently, should also be taped every time they are used. Once I got one of these small

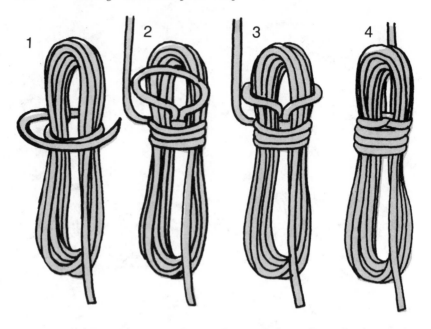

Stowing a standard coil of line. After you have coiled your line, take the remaining end and wrap it three or four times around the entire coil pulling the end through to form a loop that is dropped back over the top of the coil and then pulled tight. This keeps the coil from coming undone, and it may be stored securely in its bin.

cotter rings caught in a line that I was tightening. The ring pulled right out of the pin that it was securing. Moments later the pin dropped out and with it the shroud and mast. Be very careful. Although these rings look secure, they should be taped to keep them from coming adrift.

If you do not have to remove cotter rings frequently, the best way of securing them is just to bury them in a gob of clear silicone caulking. The caulking will adhere to both the ring and the pin, preventing the ring from coming adrift; yet, it can be removed using just your fingers if you ever have to take out the pin. Also, since it is not noticeable, it does not detract from the appearance of your boat. Be especially cautious of any cotter pin or cotter ring that is in your lifeline. You want to keep them strong and secure at all costs.

All sails, when not in use, must either be bagged or left on the boom and covered with a sail cover. Ultraviolet rays of the sun are probably the worst enemy your sails could have. Use a good quality sail cover to keep the ultraviolet rays from weakening your sail. When you put your sails in a sail bag for storage, there are two schools of thought.

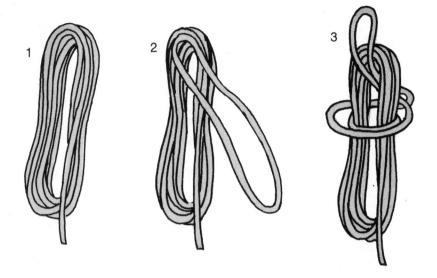

Coiling a line for hanging. After you have completed your standard coil, take any one of the loops and separate it from the main coil. Grasping the loop at the very bottom, pull it taut. Take it once or twice around the entire coil and back up through the top portion of the coil, pulling it tight. This gives you a loop so that you can hang the coil of line neatly on a peg or hook.

There are the stuffers and the folders. Some people just stuff a jib into a bag; others insist that it be folded. If you fold a sail it will take up far less room and be eaiser to get out of the bag and installed on the boat. However, there are two drawbacks to folding sails: one, you need a large, flat, clean work area to lay the sail out in order to fold it properly; two, sails tend to be folded along the same creases each time, creating an area that receives excess chafe and wear, thereby weakening the sail. In extremely light air these creases make a sail look peculiar and cause it to be inefficient as well. If you stuff your sails, you lengthen the life of the sail since the folds won't be in the same place each time. But it takes far more room to store a sail that is just stuffed in a bag.

No matter which method you use, you should put the sail in the bag so that the corner that you attach to the boat first is the last corner put into the bag. It will then be the first corner out of the bag. In the case of the jib, the tack should be right in the mouth of the sail bag. Take the drawstring from the sail bag and tie it right through the tack of the jib; as you untie the sailbag, you will have the tack right in your hand. Place the mainsail into the bag so that the clew is on top because the clew is the first part of the sail that you attach to the boat.

When furling the mainsail onto the boom, have four or five sail stops handy. Sail stops are pieces of nylon ribbon or small pieces of line that you can use to tie up the sail after you have it furled. Just before you drop your mainsail, place the sail stops between the foot of the sail and the boom, letting them hang down equidistant from either side of the boom. That way you won't have to search for them while you're trying to furl the sail. After the sail is rolled into a neat furl on top of the boom, bring each end of the sail stops under and around the boom, cross them over on top of the sail, and tie them in a plain old bowknot as you tie your shoes. This will keep the sail secured on top of the boom and keep it from sagging. It's a good idea to use colored sail stops, say a piece of line with a built-in color tracer or fully colored lines. These are available through most ship chandlers. A colored line is more visible against the white color of the sails. You won't overlook untying any stops before you try to raise the sail.

An inexpensive cotton doormat should be on any crusing boat – from the smallest to the largest racing machines. Modern deck shoes track dirt and sand onto your boat, especially if they are wet. You will find yourself constantly swabbing, trying to keep the boat clean. The judicious placement of a mat, either on the dock or on the boat where you board, will save you hours of needless scrubbing.

Winch handles also need to be stored properly on a boat. I once heard that winch handles are the only things magnetized by water; they tend to fly out of the cockpit and into the bay constantly. A winch handle holder in the cockpit of the boat will help keep the winch handle always ready where it's needed. Never leave winch handles in a winch. They are sure to jump overboard and can be quite dangerous in certain tacking situations.

If you keep a water hose or a shore power cord aboard, after you've coiled it take the two ends and screw them together. This will keep any water that's left in the hose from running out and filling the compartment. It will also keep the electric cord far neater and protect the prongs on the end from any saltwater intrusion.

Charts are very difficult to store in a small boat. Rolling charts is not satisfactory because when you unroll them you don't have a surface large enough to put them down on anyway. Most charts have to be folded. Try to put the folds in areas in which you are least likely to sail, and keep the area in which you are most likely to sail folded on the top. Along with your charts, your parallel rules, protractors, and dividers each should have a box of their own. Dividers can become a lethal weapon if they come loose and fly across the cockpit. A com-

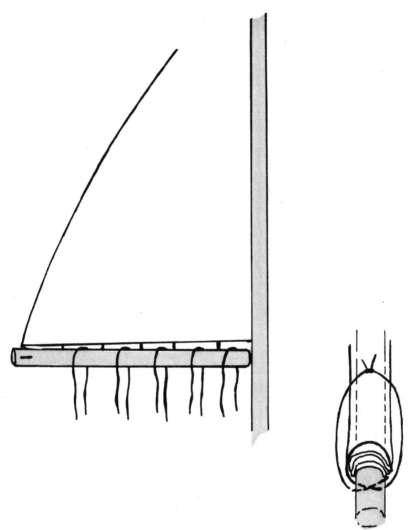

Using sail stops in furling the mainsail.

mon wine bottle cork that has been well oiled will not only keep the
points of the divider sharp and clean, and prevent them from getting
rusty, but will also prevent them from hurting anyone should they come
adrift.

Try to keep all extra gear out of the cockpit and below. If you are
scurrying around during a jibe or tack it is quite easy to step on a sweater
that's been left in the cockpit. When this happens, your deck shoes give

you marvelous traction on the sweater; but the sweater gives you zero traction on the deck, and you are liable to hurt yourself. So please, keep all extra material out of the cockpit; store it somewhere so that it won't cause accidents. One of the worst causes of falls in small boats is stepping onto the small standard cockpit cushion. Be especially careful of this.

MAINTENANCE

Maintenance requires constant vigilance on the part of the sailboat owner. Write out a checklist, just as the aviation enthusiast does for checking out his airplane every time he takes off. Check the blocks, the fittings, the shrouds, the condition of the sails, the location of the safety equipment, and whether it's all in good shape.

Winches need to be lubricated once or twice a season with light lubricant that should be water resistant. Don't use too much lubricant or it could cook in the hot sun, run out of the bottom of the winches, and get over everything. In taking the winches apart to lubricate them, be extremely careful that nothing slips out of your hand and jumps over the side; you may be without a winch until you get the replacement parts. I have found a good method to prevent this. Before you start to disassemble the winch, get a good-sized cardboard box about a foot and a half square and six inches deep. Cut a hole in it exactly the size of your winch, slip it over the winch, and then proceed to take it apart. If you drop any pieces, they will stay in the cardboard box and save you all kinds of trouble.

Blocks, fittings, and shackles should all be lubricated. There are many good silicone-based sprays on the market that are nonstaining and long lasting. The aerosal types are extremely useful for this purpose.

An area that should be checked more than once a season is the spreader tips. Make sure these are securely padded so that they don't tear either your main or your jib. This very common occurrence can be easily avoided.

While we're on the subject of sail maintenance, make sure your battens fit properly. A batten that is too long distorts the sail and quickly wears out the ends of the batten pockets. And one that is too short won't work properly. Make sure all the edges of the batten are smooth and rounded and that the battens are the proper length.

If you have an engine aboard your boat, follow the manufacturer's recommendations for maintenance. The worst and most common cause of failure in both diesel and gasoline engines is water – in the fuel

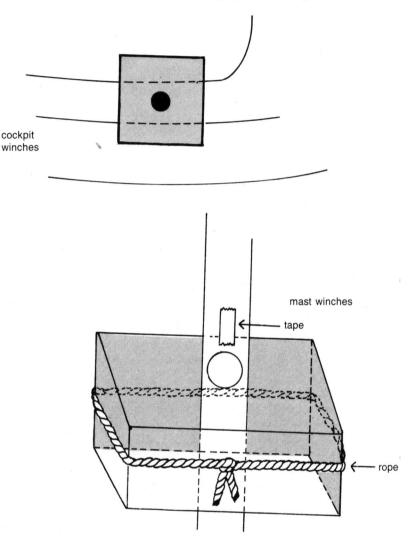

cockpit
winches

mast winches

tape

rope

Part-saver boxes used when repairing cockpit winches and mast winches.

of the diesel engine and in the fuel or the electrical system of the gasoline engine. Make sure that you have a large, efficient strainer and
water separator installed in your fuel line and that you check them
frequently.

Freshwater strainers should be checked frequently; any grass or
foreign matter that impedes the flow of water to cool the engine should

be removed. Since water comes out of the exhaust system of your engine, look at how much water is coming out every time you turn on your engine. You will soon learn to recognize the amount of water that is normally discharged from your engine's cooling system. If there's any deviation from this, you can quickly find out why and correct the problem before the engine overheats.

I like the sonic alarms that sound on an engine if the water temperature gets too high or if the oil pressure gets too low. The nice thing about the sonic alarms is that you don't have to look at your gauges all the time. On many boats the gauges are located in inaccessible areas or are completely absent. Another advantage is that each time you turn the key to start the engine, the sonic alarms sound, giving you a daily check on whether or not they're operating. If the low-oil pressure sounder doesn't go off when you turn on the key, it should be fixed immediately. You cannot tell as easily whether ordinary oil gauges work.

Alcohol stoves are the most common way of cooking on small cruising boats, and they should be handled with great respect. If there is any malfunction or if you should accidently overprime the stove, alcohol fires are easy to put out. Follow the manufacturer's instructions to the letter when using the stove. But before you even attempt to light the stove, fill a pan with water and put it next to the stove. If anything should happen, all you have to do is dump the pan of water onto the fire to put it out before any damage can occur. Also, water is far easier to clean up than the discharge from a fire extinguisher.

Electrical systems on boats are like electrical systems anywhere: they don't mix with salt water. Keep all electric wire up and out of the bilges, keep your electrical box and battery dry, and keep the water level in the batteries constant. Three or four times a season spray all electrical components with one of the silicone sealer-type lubricants to try to keep moisture out of the system.

There are many methods of treating the wooden trim on a modern, fiberglass sailboat. Nothing looks prettier than several coats of marine spar varnish, shiny enough to reflect your image. If you have a small boat that you can take home and put in your garage and work on in the off season, by all means use a good quality marine spar varnish, and you will have yourself a mini yacht. Varnishing in the heat of the summer when everyone else is out sailing isn't all that much fun. So if you want to, you can save time by using one of the modern teak cleaners. Do follow the manufacturer's instructions. Since these teak cleaners are usually quite caustic, it is important to wear gloves. After cleaning the teak, there are dozens of teak oils and finishes on the market that you can choose from. Check with your neighbors in the marina or your club to find out what they are using because many products are far more satisfactory in certain climates than others. Teak finish that would work well in colder New England may not be satisfactory at all in the heat of the tropics.

Sailors have been finishing and protecting wooden trim in boats for so many years that almost everyone has come up with his own pet method. Don't listen to them. Read the instructions on the can and follow the manufacturer's instructions. Since chemists with years of experience have done the research, why disregard the instructions and listen to the retired shoe salesman who has the boat in the next slip. If you want real satisfaction in maintaining and finishing your bright work, plan on working at it. There are no shortcuts. It sure looks pretty when it's all done well.

The modern fiberglass hull does not need bottom paint to protect it from the environment; it needs a bottom paint to keep growth from adhering to the boat and slowing it down. When boats were all made of wood, worms and parasites would bore right into the wood. We haven't developed a fiberglass-eating bug yet, but even in freshwater lakes, grass and algae will adhere to the bottom of the boat, considerably hampering its ability to sail fast. Which bottom paint you use depends on how you use your boat, the area in which you sail most often, and the size of your boat.

If you trailer your boat and put it in for a weekend or a week at the most, bottom paint is not really necessary because the grass and barnacles won't grow that fast. When you haul your boat out and lash it to the trailer, a quick freshwater rinse of the bottom will have it shipshape again. However, if you launch your boat in the spring and keep it in the water the entire summer season or keep it in year-round— whether you're in fresh or salt water—some sort of toxic bottom paint is required.

Again, check with your neighbors. The bottom paint that is effective in tropical water may not be as effective in northern, cooler, fresh water. Bottom paint, with its high percentage of copper, can cost quite a bit and may not be necessary in northern waters. As a rule of thumb, the higher the water temperature, the saltier the water, and the more fouling that will occur. Southern salt water is more prone to be foul than brackish baywater such as in the Chesapeake or cooler fresh water such as in the Great Lakes.

Before you purchase bottom paint, consider how much swimming you do off your vessel. If you use a soft-finish bottom paint, every time you brush up against it while you're swimming a large patch of paint will come off the bottom and onto your arm. This can be quite annoying. Hard-finish bottom paint might be more to your liking.

The topside and decks of your fiberglass boat should have the salt water and salt spray washed off them each time you use them. At least once each season a good coat of some type of fiberglass polish or wax should be applied to keep the boat looking young longer.

The darker the color of your boat, the more pronounced the fading will be. If your boat is trailerable, try to park it in the shade; this will retard the fading process and keep the boat looking new far longer.

Anodized aluminum masts should be sprayed at least once a season with a protective aluminum coating. Although you can get this product through most marine chandlers, many hardware stores sell the same stuff at half the price for use on aluminum window frames and sashes.

Stainless steel pulpits and stanchions can be polished with any of the commercial stainless steel polishes.

I'm not going to cover the maintenance of marine heads; there are too many types on the market that have completely different maintenance requirements. When in doubt, follow the manufacturer's instructions. Remember, there are no plumbers at sea to fix your stopped-up toilet.

REVIEW QUESTIONS

(Answers follow part 7)

1. What should you use for a stopper knot and why?
2. Why should dock lines not have permanent eye splices in them?
3. Which is a longer lasting whipping – a needle whipping or a common whipping?
4. Why should cotter pins be covered with tape?
5. In stowing your mainsail in a bag, which corner should be last in, first out?
6. How often should you lubricate your winches?
7. How often should you check your strainers?
8. What should you do before lighting an alcohol stove?
9. Do all boats need bottom paint?
10. Don't you wish you were out sailing right now?

SAILING EXERCISE V

Get a piece of line about six feet long and practice knot tying. Make sure you can tie the square or reef knot, figure eight knot, the bowline, and the clove hitch without having to think about it. Tie them over and over again until you are able to do it in the dark.

The next part of this exercise is putting to practical use what you've learned in this chapter. Check your boat over and make sure that all of the lines are whipped — not just burnt on the end but whipped with either the common whipping or a needle whipping.

Make sure all of the cotter rings and cotter pins are taped so that they do not snag either your flesh or your clothing.

Practice coiling your halyards and mooring lines and anchor lines. And figure out which system of stowing them is best to use in your boat.

Refold your sails and place them in the bag so that the proper corner can be located quickly as you remove them from the bag.

Check your winches and make sure they are properly lubricated. It is surprising how many times a new boat will leave the factory without proper lubrication in the winches.

Take your silicone-based spray and spray all of the blocks, shackles, snaps, and fittings.

If you have an engine aboard your boat, check the water and fuel strainers; make sure they're clean. Learn how to open and close your thru-hull valves.

Check the location and the service date on all of your fire extinguishers. Check your electrical fuses and switches, and check your battery for water level. Take your sealer-lubricant and spray the battery terminals to keep them free of corrosion.

Spray the aluminum mast and boom and any other aluminum fittings with one of your aluminum protective coatings.

Now step back and admire your handiwork. Not only are you learning to sail but you're learning to keep your boat shipshape.

Additional Sails and Masts

In the first five parts of this book, we discussed only single-masted vessels – sloops – with only a main and jib. We are now going to cover additional sails, such as spinnakers and staysails. We are also going to discuss multi-masted vessels, such as ketches, yawls, and schooners. The sails that apply to these multi-masted vessels are very similar to those that we have described for our single-masted sloop with its jib and mainsail alone.

TWO MORE SAILS

Staysails

In its broadest definition, a staysail is a sail that is attached to a stay. Traditionally, staysails are flown like a mini jib, slightly aft of your jib. A staysail is trimmed exactly as a jib is trimmed. Remember your early sailing lessons? The first sail you trim is the first one affected by the wind – that is, the furthest sail forward. When you are setting

A sloop.

your staysail properly, you first trim the jib, then the jib staysail, followed by the mainsail; as each sail spills the wind out of it, it will affect
the sail that is behind it.

   Vessels with a jib, a staysail, and a mainsail are commonly called
cutters. I have discovered that the easiest way to differentiate between
a cutter and a sloop is to ask the man who owns the boat. Because they
are so similar in size – and both of them can fly staysails – it is almost
at the discretion of the owner whether he wishes to call his vessel a
cutter or a sloop. Usually, the main mast on a cutter is slightly further
aft than the main mast on a sloop. But this is not always true. When
in doubt, ask the man who owns it.

A cutter.

Spinnakers

The one additional sail that you will see frequently is the spinnaker. The spinnaker is the large balloon-shaped sail that bellows out in front of the boat almost like a parachute – sometimes, in fact, they are called chutes – to propel the boat downwind or on a broad reach. A spinnaker can also be flown on a beam reach. The closer you come into the wind, however, the less efficient the spinnaker becomes and the more efficient a plain jib or a genoa would be. So there becomes a point of trade-off depending on your vessel, wind velocity, and many other things.

The spinnaker is probably the most romantic, photogenic, and cursed sail that you will ever have on your boat. Flying a spinnaker

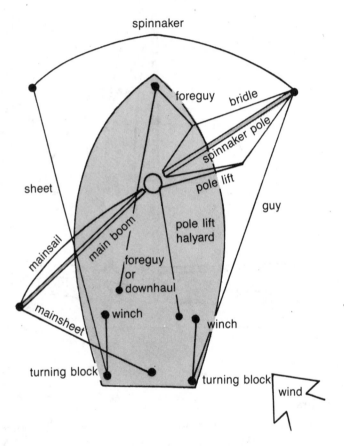

Spinnaker rigging.

takes skill, coordination, and cooperation. Don't ever attempt to set a spinnaker without plenty of room and competent help.

To fly a spinnaker you need a whole set of added equipment: a spinnaker halyard; a pole lift halyard; a spinnaker pole; a pole foreguy, or downhaul; a spinnaker sheet and a spinnaker guy—which are interchangeable; special spinnaker sheet blocks; a spinnaker track or eye on the fore side of the mast; and, of course, the spinnaker. If you are fortunate enough to have this additional equipment installed on your boat, you'll need a brief rundown on how to use it.

The spinnaker is for off-wind sailing only. When you are moving downwind, the main is already out. The spinnaker is always set opposite the main to capture the maximum amount of air while running; it is drawn closer to the same side as the main when the boat is sailed closer to the wind – in broad reaching, for instance.

The function of the spinnaker pole, which is always set opposite and parallel to the main boom, is to hold out one corner of the triangular sail and help it keep its shape; that corner, or clew, is secured through the outboard jaw of the pole by a line or afterguy. The head of the spinnaker is secured to a halyard for raising the sail; the other clew is attached to a sheet which controls the spinnaker trim. For normal small boat rigging, there are two other lines, both of which control the spinnaker pole: a pole lift halyard for raising and taking the weight of the pole off the sail; and the downhaul, or foreguy, for helping to keep the pole in position.

When rigging the spinnaker, remember that all trimming lines (sheet, afterguy, etc.) run outside of everything since the spinnaker flies forward of the forestay. When raising the spinnaker, the genoa remains up. The halyard is then quickly hoisted while some tension is kept on the guy and sheet to open the sail and get it drawing. Once up, the pole is put into proper position by pulling it aft with the guy so that the pole is perpendicular to the apparent wind. The sheet must be let out enough so that there will be a slight curl in the luff of the spinnaker – but not so much that it collapses. The genoa should come down quickly and immediately so that it will not drown the spinnaker in its shadow.

Jibing the Chute

Tacking downwind under spinnaker can only be accomplished by jibing. The boat must be directed to the other tack, and the chute must be jibed in order to do so. The maneuver need not be a fearsome experience. Jibing the chute is a form of sail handling that the crew and skipper can learn to do as a matter of routine. If the cruising skipper plans to use a spinnaker at all, he must learn to jibe it; otherwise, the usefulness and enjoyment of this off-wind sail will be blunted. As in all sail-handling procedures, organization, preparation, and practice are the keys. Once learned, jibing the chute becomes a functional part of sailing.

To jibe the chute on a small boat properly, you should have a minimum of three in crew. Small boat jibing usually uses the end-for-end pole system; one person on the foredeck handles the pole and orders sheet and guy release and trim. In the cockpit, the helmsman steers and controls one sheet or guy; the other crewman is responsible for taking in and letting out the main and the other sheet or guy, plus the downhaul if necessary. Before the command for jibing is given, all lines are checked. It is good practice for the foredeck man to bring the spinnaker sheet to the mast before he unhooks the pole.

When the crew is ready and in place, the helmsman calls, "Jibing," and the main is sheeted in so that it will not blanket the spinnaker. The boat must now be steered directly downwind so that the spinnaker can be kept full and drawing. The downhaul must be released from its cleat. Appropriate sheets and guys are eased or taken in so that the spinnaker is kept full, while the pole, theoretically, is at a right angle to the boat's fore-and-aft line. Now, the foredeckman unsnaps the inboard end of the pole from the mast and snaps that end on the sheet, which becomes the new guy. Then he unsnaps the pole from the original guy and snaps that end to the mast.

As the main is jibed and let out and the boat is steered onto the new tack, the guy and new sheet are trimmed accordingly. Although this maneuver is simple, it's also very easy to do incorrectly. I suggest that you have competent help and, for the first few times, do it only in light wind with the boat securely tied to the dock by the stern.

MULTI-MASTED VESSELS

The next step up in complexity from a cutter is two-masted vessels of three different kinds—ketches, yawls, and schooners. In ketches and yawls, the foremast is taller than the aftermast. The aftermast is called the mizen mast and flies a triangular mini mainsail like the one on your mainmast. In a ketch, the mizen mast is set forward of the rudder post of the vessel; in a yawl, it is set behind the rudder post of the vessel.

Ketches

Today there are far more ketches than yawls; on a ketch, the three chief sails—the jib, the mainsail, and the mizen—are far closer to each other in area. This gives you the advantage of, let's say, a boat that has approximately 600 square feet of sail in total area, having approximately a 200-square foot jib, a 200-square foot main, and a 200-square foot mizen. This way you can handle each 200-foot sail independently and either reef them or douse them with impending storms without needing a great deal of strength. If the same amount of sail area were on a sloop,

A ketch.

with its main and jib, you would have 300 square feet of sail in each sail. In deteriorating weather, it would require more strength to handle 300 square feet of sail than it would to handle the smaller sails.

Another distinct advantage to the ketch or yawl rig is that you can reef very easily by dropping the mainsail and sailing with just the jib and mizen – commonly called sailing with just jib and jigger – and the boat will still be in balance. You have a large piece of sail forward to force you out of the wind and you have a large piece of sail in the mizen to force you back up into the wind. You can sail this way as the wind increases and the boat will still be balanced very nicely.

Yawls

Yawls have basically the same conformation as ketches. The mizen, however, is usually much smaller than the mizen on a ketch. And the

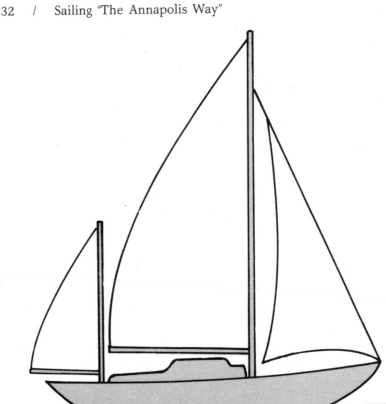

A yawl.

advantages of having the divided rig – or two masts – are not quite as pronounced. On ketches and yawls, staysails can also be flown between the masts from the top of the mizen mast and tacked forward. These are called mizen staysails. Now, we're getting into more exotic sails that are normally used only for racing; so we'll just leave it there.

Schooners

Schooners are also two-masted vessels. In a schooner, however, both of the masts are either exactly the same height or the forward mast is slightly shorter than the aftermast. The forward mast is called the foremast; the aftermast is called the main mast. On the fore side of the forward mast you will have your jib and your staysail, if desired. On the after side you will have your foresail, which is nothing more than a mini mainsail. On the fore side of your main mast you can have another staysail, and on the after side, a large mainsail.

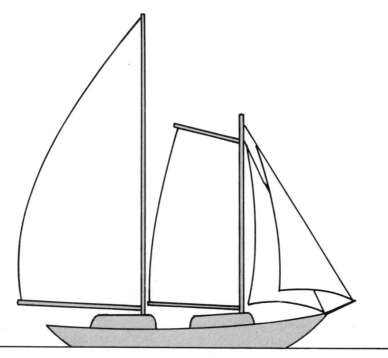

A schooner.

The schooner rig was developed early in the history of our country; a very small crew could handle a lot of sail on a vessel that had good cargo-carrying capacity and could sail to windward far better than the old square-rigged vessels could. There are very few modern schooners being built today. The development of stainless steel shrouds, aluminum masts, and Dacron sails makes it far simpler to have two or three sails on a boat than five or six.

REVIEW QUESTIONS
[Answers follow part 7]

1. Which sail do you trim first – the jib, the staysail, or the mainsail?
2. What is the difference between a cutter and a sloop?
3. What is the difference between a ketch and a yawl?
4. How do you tell the difference between a schooner and a ketch or a yawl?
5. On what points of sailing do you use a spinnaker?
6. In what position should the spinnaker pole be in relation to the wind?

7. In what position should the spinnaker pole be in relation to the main boom?
8. In rigging the spinnaker, where do the sheets and guys go?
9. What is the minimum number of people there should be before you use a spinnaker?
10. Explain the difference between the spinnaker sheet and a guy.

SAILING EXERCISE VI

We will limit this practice session to the use of the spinnaker. Choose a day when there are very light winds, and practice with the boat tied securely in the slip, anchored by the stern, or still on the trailer. Proceed in the following manner.

With the stern pointing into the wind, raise the mainsail and the jib. You will find it difficult to raise the mainsail since you are not pointing into the wind, but, with patience, you can raise it. Trim the main sail as you would when running.

It is now time to rig and raise the spinnaker. When you have the spinnaker up and full, lower the jib and secure it on deck. Practice moving the pole forward and back and up and down. Notice how, every time you move the pole, you have to change the position of the spinnaker sheet as well. Move the boat slightly so that the wind is dead astern. Jibe both the mainsail and the spinnaker by removing the spinnaker pole from the eye on the mast and attaching it to the spinnaker at the old sheet location. Detach the pole from the old guy and attach it to the eye on the mast.

Next the sails should be trimmed and the pole set properly. The old sheet is now your guy; the old guy is now your sheet. Repeat this jibing operation several times until it becomes automatic.

Now take the spinnaker down. We do this by first raising the jib and then releasing the spinnaker guy. This lets the sail fly around the forestay. By pulling on the sheet and gathering in the sail in the wind shadow of the main and jib, you can lower the halyard and easily lower your spinnaker.

A word of caution: if you are practicing these maneuvers with the boat on the trailer, be sure the boat is securely tied to both the trailer and the ground.

You are now ready to go out and sail downwind with your spinnaker. Remember, there must be at least a crew of three. And don't attempt to set the spinnaker the first few times in anything but steady light breezes.

7

Good Seamanship

RULES OF THE ROAD

To promote safety in navigation, Congress enacted a set of requirements called Rules of the Road. We will cover only the rules that apply to a typical small sailboat and the small powerboats that you are likely to encounter.

Rules of the Road cover steering and sailing rules, sound signals for both good and restricted visibility, and distress signals. Since we do not advocate sailing in limited visibility, we will cover only the portion of the rules that involve crossing, approaching, and overtaking situations with sailboats and powerboats. There are three chief sets of rules: the Inland Rules, used on inland waters of the United States; the International Rules, which are used offshore internationally, and the Western Lakes and Rivers Rules, which are used on certain inland lakes and rivers.

Almost all of the right-of-way rules have as their basis that the less maneuverable of the two boats is granted the right-of-way. When two boats are of equal size and equal maneuverability, we must make some sort of determination as to who has the right-of-way.

In our first situation, two boats – A and B – are making a standard crossing at almost right angles to each other. I have found that the easiest way to remember who has the right-of-way in a crossing situation is to remember how your navigation lights are positioned on the boat. If you can see the red light on the port bow of the approaching boat, you are in the danger zone and are classified as the give-way vessel. You must change your course and give way to the other boat – called the stand-on vessel – who is privileged to stand on his course and continue on his way. When he looks at your vessel, he will see the green light on your starboard bow and know that he has the go-ahead, or green light.

When two powerboats meet approximately head-on, as often happens in a narrow channel, both boats should turn slightly to the right so that they pass port side to port side. This is the same thing that occurs on the highway. You keep to the right. It's just plain common sense.

When two powerboats are overtaking each other, the overtaken vessel – or slower boat – has the right-of-way. The approaching boat must change course and go either to his right or left. As on the highway, it is normal to pass to the left. It is not illegal, however, to pass to the right-hand side of the boat that you are overtaking. All of these rules apply in both inland and international waters.

When a sailboat and a powerboat meet, an entirely different set of rules applies. Again, the rules favor the less maneuverable of the two boats. Since a sailboat is usually less maneuverable than a powerboat, a sailboat will normally have the right-of-way. In the illustration of a powerboat and a sailboat crossing, the sailboat is in the powerboat's danger zone, or red zone. The sailboat, however, still has the right-of-way because he is under sail alone and is, therefore, less maneuverable.

It is safe to say that a sailboat has the right-of-way over a powerboat at all times except for situations in which the powerboat is less maneuverable. These exceptions include vessels engaged in fishing or dredging, or vessels restricted to a narrow channel because of their draft. Again, it's just common sense. A boat that has all of its fishing nets out cannot possibly maneuver as well as your small sailboat; so you must stay out of his way.

One interesting exception to the above rule is the situation in which the sailboat is overtaking the powerboat from astern. Realistically, this seldom happens since most powerboats are much faster than sailboats. It could happen, however, when a powerboat slows down on entering a harbor and a sailboat comes in with a good breeze right behind him. The overtaken boat, or the powerboat, has the right-of-way; the sailboat

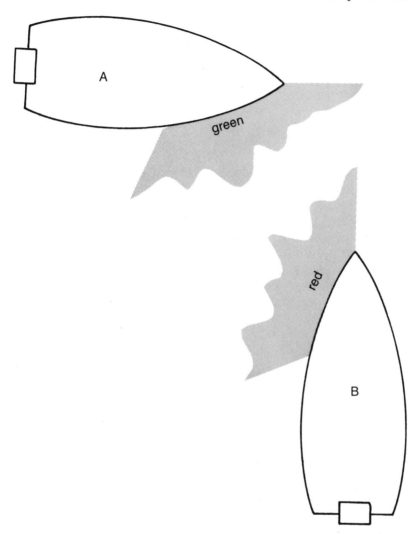

Powerboat crossing situation. Boat B has the right-of-way as boat A is approaching from his red danger zone.

must stay clear. Again, it's the same thing as on the highway. You are not allowed to come up and smash into somebody's trunk. I guarantee you that this question will appear on almost every test on right-of-way rules because it is a rather tricky exception.

When two sailboats meet, all of the rules relate to wind direction and to which tack the boat is sailing on. It's easy to say that the star-

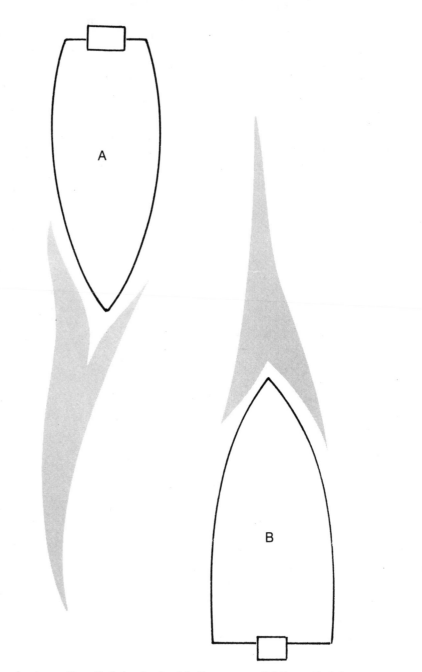

Powerboats meeting. Both boats should alter course slightly so that they pass port side to port side.

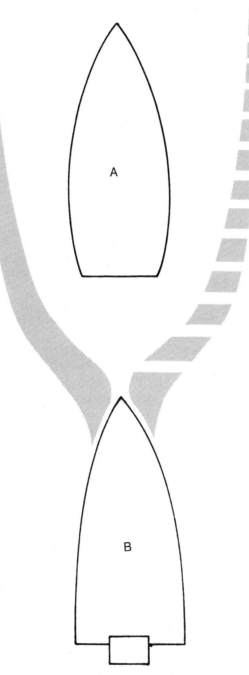

Powerboats overtaking each other. Although it is legal for boat B to pass boat A on either side, it is normally done to the left as on the highway.

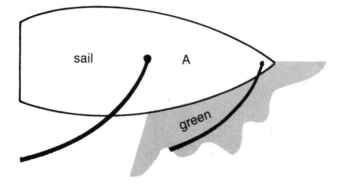

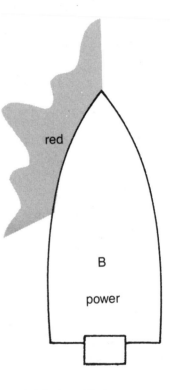

Powerboat and a sailboat crossing. Although boat A is in boat B's danger zone, boat A has the right-of-way because he is a sailboat and therefore less maneuverable.

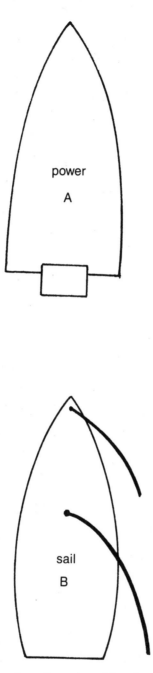

Sailboat overtaking a powerboat. Powerboat A has the right-of-way because boat B is overtaking him and therefore required to stand clear.

board tack boat always has the right-of-way over the port tack boat; and in 99 out of 100 situations, this is true. When each boat approaches at approximately 90 degrees to each other, one boat beating to windward on the port tack and the other beating to windward on the starboard tack, the starboard tack boat always has the right-of-way. This is an arbitrary ruling since there is no difference in the two boats' maneuverability.

The starboard-tack-over-port-tack privilege began years ago. In the

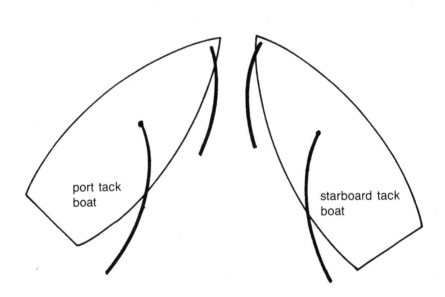

Crossing situation involving sailboats on opposite tacks. The starboard tack boat has right-of-way over the port tack vessel.

days of square riggers, the tack of the square rig sail was actually to starboard; the helmsman, who was steering from the starboard, or steer-board, side of the boat, had restricted visibility. Therefore, he had the right-of-way over the port tack boat.

When two sailboats are approaching on the same tack, the boat that is downwind, or, theoretically, in the wind shadow of the other boat, has the right-of-way. Again, right-of-way is given to the less maneuver-able boat – the boat in the wind shadow. A boat being overtaken from behind by a faster vessel is privileged, exactly as the powerboat is, to keep the faster vessel from coming up from behind and causing a collision.

With these few basic rules, you can avoid colliding in even the most crowded situations. Be careful in determining which set of rules ap-plies. At times, many racing sailors confuse racing right-of-way rules with navigation rules. Although they are similar in their basic points, racing rules are much more detailed and have far more exceptions, such as overlaps and tacking too close to a mark. I strongly suggest that, if you intend to race, the first few times you race with experienced rac-ing sailors who can explain the complexities of the racing rules to you. And there are many good books written on racing rules.

When you're sailing, you must remember: *if you turn on your engine at any time, you immediately become a powerboat, and your right-of-way responsibilities change.* Even if you still have your sails up and are motor sailing you have the full responsibilities of a powerboat to stay out of the way of sailboats, except in rare circumstances.

This covers the major points of right-of-way rules in crossing, approaching, and overtaking situations. Remember, a collision at sea can spoil everything.

BASIC YACHTING ETIQUETTE

The laws about avoiding collisions don't go far enough into some of the accepted courtesies and practices among good sailors. In over-taking another boat, a situation arises in which the faster boat has the option of passing the boat ahead of him either to windward or to leeward. As a courtesy, he should always pass to leeward. He has the faster boat. He will be able to get through the wind shadow of the boat ahead of him without slowing down much; it's just the courteous thing to do – to pass through the other boat's wind shadow and go on your way. He'll appreciate it. You'll make friends by doing this. If you are racing, of course, the only thing to do is to put the other boat in your wind shadow. After all, you want to slow him down as much as pos-

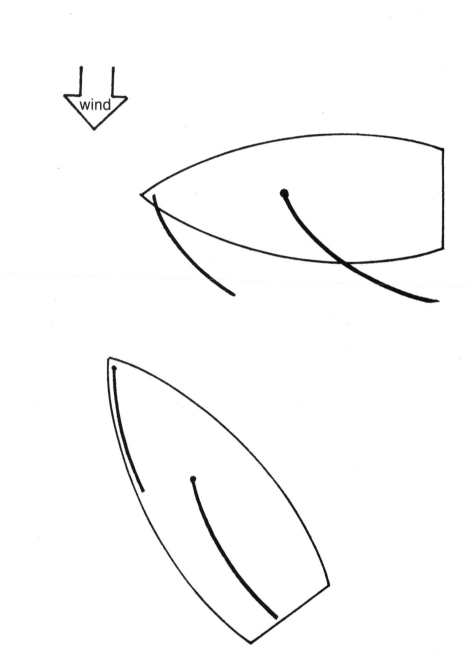

Boats crossing when both boats are on the same tack. When two sailboats approach on the same tack, the downwind boat has the right-of-way.

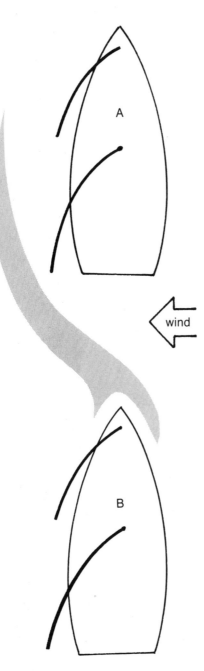

Sailboats overtaking each other from astern. Boat A has the right-of-way and boat B must maneuver to avoid collision.

sible so that you can move ahead quicker. The only exception I can see to passing to leeward is if your mother-in-law happens to be on the boat that you're passing. Then it's perfectly permissible to pass to windward.

Along the same lines, please stay clear of racing boats when you are out for just a nice afternoon sail. Some racing clubs are now displaying identifying flags on their boats to show that they are racing. Although this does not give them the right-of-way, it's just plain courteous to stay out of their way if you can. And remember, your sails will throw a wind shadow downwind from you approximately 10 times the distance that your mast is high. If your mast is 30 feet off the water, you will throw disturbed air 300 feet downwind, or approximately the length of a football field.

Many people have started to sail in order to gain some privacy. Since the waterways get more crowded every year, it is harder to find secluded anchorages where you can retain your privacy. If you approach an anchorage where there are other boats, make sure you are far enough away so that you don't drop your anchor over their anchor line; if you anchor too close and the wind changes direction, you will be sitting on top of each other—or worse yet, bumping in the night.

Once a boat came in, anchored directly to windward of us, and then started a very large fire in his barbecue on the stern of his boat. The sparks drifted down on us, followed by the smell of his burning chicken. That was one of the worst nights I ever spent at anchor. Please try to stay clear when anchoring.

People are out there to enjoy a quiet night in a secluded anchorage. If you are playing your electric guitar or bongo drums, please keep the volume down so that it doesn't disturb the other boats in the anchorage. As with the right-of-way rules, it's just common courtesy.

A bugaboo for many sailors is their first entrance into a strange marina. Where do you go? Who do you see? How do you know where to tie up? Many marinas will be monitoring the ship-to-shore radio; if your boat is so equipped, you can sometimes get information that way. If you do not have a radio and you can't attract attention, your best bet is to head for the gas dock where the transient boats can pull in and gas up. Tie your vessel there temporarily and try to find the dockmaster for a slip assignment. If you can't find anybody, move down to the far end of the gas dock to leave the pumps open for others. Don't leave your boat; somebody will be down shortly to take care of you.

Always check the marina's requirements when you tie up. Many of the nicest marinas have restrictions against hanging towels and wet bathing suits on the boat. And, of course, find out where you should deposit your trash if this is allowed. Many marinas on out-of-the-way islands have no facilities for handling trash. It is far easier to carry it with you to the next marina and deposit it ashore than it is for them to gather it and carry it ashore in their work boats. I can't repeat often enough: just be considerate. As the waterways get more crowded, we all have to work harder and harder to maintain a joyous sailing atmosphere.

REVIEW QUESTIONS

(Answers follow part 7)

1. Is a boat under sail with its engine engaged a sailboat or powerboat under the rules?
2. Under what circumstances does a powerboat have the right-of-way over a sailboat?
3. When two sailboats approach on opposite tacks who has the right-of-way?
4. When two sailboats approach on the same tack who has the right-of-way?
5. Where should you usually go for information when entering a strange marina?

Answers to Review Questions

PART 1

1. An airfoil shape in the sail, a keel or centerboard, and a difference of air pressure on either side of the sail.
2. Centerboard, leeboard, and daggerboard.
3. The swing keel should be locked all the way down at all times when sailing.
4. To promote stability and to keep the boat from sliding sideways.
5. A sail is a sail; a sheet is a line or rope that trims the sail in or leaves it out.
6. a) A lifejacket for each person aboard plus a type IV device for throwing.
   b) A fire extinguisher if there is an engine.
   c) A whistle.
   d) A set of distress signals.
7. The mainsail.
8. The tapered end.
9. The tack.

10. The figure eight knot.
11. Check that the boat is pointing into the wind.
12. Appoximately abeam.
13. Let them out.
14. Into the wind.
15. Into the sail.
16. Point it into the wind.

PART 2

1. Trim the sails as flat as possible *without destroying the airfoil shape*.
2. The telltales or wind indicator, the sails for luffing, and the course you are sailing.
3. It is a rapid series of very short tacks and come abouts.
4. A whisker pole.
5. Sailing wing and wing.
6. The stern.
7. The mainsail.
8. Anchor and then ease out the anchor line till you're ashore.
9. Enough forward speed to have water passing over the rudder.
10. Only if the wind is from such a direction that you can easily sail out again.

PART 3

1. Throw something that floats overboard.
2. Jibe.
3. The jib will be full of scallops.
4. The bottom third along the luff.
5. The top third along the luff.
6. The sail is stretched and the airfoil shape is destroyed or distorted.
7. It allows more adjustment to the shape of the mainsail.
8. It keeps the boom from lifting.
9. A small anchor used for short anchoring stops in good weather.
10. Moving your hand up and down, palm down.

PART 4

1. Sail trim, centerboard position or crew weight distribution, and heeling.
2. The point at which a boat may be hauled laterally and still stay perpendicular to the line of pull, commonly called the pivot point.

3. The point in the sails where all the wind effort seems to concentrate its force.
4. Out of the wind.
5. Out of the wind.
6. Out of the wind.
7. Into the wind.
8. Running downwind.
9. Take a compass site on a landmark before the rain sets in; sail a known compass course; anchor if you don't know where you are.
10. Reduce sail area.
11. As tight as possible.
12. Very loose so that there is no strain on the sail.
13. Keep the boat from turning upside down.
14. Turn the hull so that the mast is pointing into the wind. The wind will push the boat and pull the mast out of the mud.

PART 5

1. The figure eight knot because it is easy to untie.
2. The plain line is more versatile. A knotted loop can be untied and a straight line run through a block.
3. A needle whipping.
4. To protect you and your sails from their sharp edges.
5. The clew.
6. At least once a season.
7. Daily.
8. Draw a pan of water.
9. No, only boats left in the water for an extended period of time.
10. Yes, yes, yes!

PART 6

1. The first sail affected by the wind – the jib.
2. Very little. A cutter has its mast stepped farther aft than a sloop.
3. The mizen sail on a yawl is much smaller and the mizen mast is farther aft than on a ketch.
4. The forward mast on a schooner is always the same height as or shorter than the after mast.
5. Reaching and running.
6. It should be perpendicular to it.
7. It should be parallel to it.
8. Outside all of the shrouds and lifelines and forward of the forestay.

9. At least three.
10. These lines are identical but their names change with their function. The guy goes to the outboard end of the pole and the tack of the spinnaker while the sheet goes to the clew of the spinnaker. When the spinnaker is jibed, the function of these lines changes along with their names. The sheet becomes the guy and the guy becomes the sheet.

PART 7

1. Powerboat.
2. When the powerboat has restricted maneuverability due to fishing, towing, dredging, etc., or when the powerboat is being overtaken from astern.
3. The starboard tack boat.
4. The downwind boat.
5. The gas dock.

Glossary

This list is intended to familiarize you with some of the words that you may be using. Do not try to memorize the terms. They will become second nature to you, and many you may already know.

A sailor starts and ends with the wind:
    LEE, LEEWARD, DOWNWIND – away from the wind.
    WINDWARD, WEATHER, UPWIND – toward the wind.

Some important parts of the boat include:
    BALLAST – a weight fastened to the keel to give the boat stability.
    BEAM – the widest part of the hull.
    BOTTOM – the hull below the waterline.
    BOW – front end.
    CLEAT – a fitting to which you fasten a line.
    COCKPIT – a recessed area in the deck where you sit.
    DECK – the top of the boat where you walk.
    FAIRLEAD BLOCK – a pulley mounted on the deck.
    HULL – the main body of the boat.

KEEL – a structure member of wood or metal projecting downward from the bottom of the boat.

PORT – left side facing forward.

RUDDER – a device to which the tiller is attached to allow the boat to be steered.

STARBOARD – right side facing forward.

STERN – back end.

TILLER – a lever attached to the rudder so that you can control it.

WINCH – a device for "snubbing" or taking the strain on a line.

The spars:

BOOM – a spar attached to the mast to which the foot of the sail is attached.

MAST – the vertical pole to which the sails are fastened.

Standing rigging is made of wire or cable and includes:

BACKSTAY – runs from masthead to the stern.

FORESTAY – runs from masthead to the bow.

SHROUD – runs from the mast to each side.

SPREADER – holds the shrouds away from the mast.

TOPPING LIFT – supports the boom when the sail is not hoisted.

Running rigging is usually made of Dacron rope and includes:

DOWNHAUL – line that pulls down a sail.

HALYARD – line that hoists and lowers a sail.

OUTHAUL – line that pulls out a sail.

SHEET – line that controls the angle of a sail to the wind.

Most sails are triangular. The larger one is the mainsail; the smaller one forward is the jib. Major parts of the sails are:

BATTEN – strip of wood or fiberglass used to stiffen the back edge of a sail.

BOLT ROPE – a reinforcing rope sewn into the foot and luff of a sail.

CLEW – the lower back corner.

FOOT – the bottom edge, between tack and clew.

HEAD – the top corner.

LEECH – the back edge, between clew and head.

LUFF – the front edge, between head and tack.

TACK – the lower front corner.

Miscellaneous, useful words and phrases – sailing has an almost infinite number of them. You may find these handy:

AGROUND – stuck on the bottom.

BOOM CRUTCH – a crutch used to support the boom when sails are not raised.

CAST OFF – to release or untie a line.

COMING ABOUT – steering the boat into and through the wind, bow first.

DRAFT – depth the boat sits in the water.

FLAKING A LINE – laying a line down in a series of loops so that it will run free without tangling.

JIBE – same as coming about, but turning so that the stern crosses the wind.

LUFFING – fluttering of a sail along its front edge.

MAN OVERBOARD – self-explanatory.

TO MOOR – to tie up to dock or buoy.

REACHING – sailing across the wind.

RUNNING – sailing with the wind.

TACKING or BEATING – zigzagging against the wind.

TELLTALE – yarn fastened to the shrouds to show wind direction.

Index